Contents

KU-505-097

MANAGEMENT IN COLLEGES SERIES

DEVELOPING INTERPERSONAL SKILLS

By Colin Turner

ISSN 0264-5599   ISBN 0-907659-22-5

Published by The Further Education Staff College
Coombe Lodge, Blagdon, Bristol BS18 6RG
Telephone (0761) 62503

Produced by Avonset, Midsomer Norton, Bath

Preface

This book has been written primarily for staff in further education colleges though it should also be of relevance to anyone concerned with the improvement of interpersonal skills. It is not written for those who already have some training and experience in the skills of social behaviour or who are professionally employed as counsellors, psychotherapists, or group trainers.

It is an introductory volume for those who wish to begin to explore the subject of interpersonal skills.

Certain parts of the book have been drawn from an earlier Coombe Lodge publication **Interpersonal Skills in Further Education**. Chapters 1, 6, 7 and 12 are revisions of work from that book. The remaining ten chapters are entirely new.

The plan of the book is as follows:

The first chapter outlines the basic assumptions which inform our view of interpersonal skills and lists nine first-order skills of social interaction.

The following eight chapters are primarily focussed on face-to-face interactions of two people. Chapters 2-4 contain the key theoretical presentation through an exposition of Transactional Analysis. It is put forward as a particularly effective way of understanding social interactions and personal relationships and these three chapters underwrite all the others in the book. The remaining chapters in this first half are concerned with assertiveness and various aspects of counselling.

The second part of the book, chapters 10-12, looks at some aspects of group behaviour with particular emphasis on the work group.

Chapter 13 explores some of the issues and practices in sensitivity and awareness training.

AUTHOR'S NOTE

In writing the book I received helpful advice and comment from many colleagues. I owe special thanks for their careful reading of the text, their critical comment and their suggestions for improvements to Penny Chadwick of the College for the Distributive Trades, and Philippa Andrews, a former colleague. Chapter 7 incorporates some work from Jean Brookes of Thameside College of Technology. Chapter 8 is closely modelled on a paper by Russ Curtis of the British Columbia Institute of Technology and former associate tutor at the Further Education Staff College. I can take little credit for it. Many of the ideas in the book have been freely plagiarised from many sources and I have tried to acknowledge them where it seemed proper to do so. The guides to further reading at the end of each chapter are my subjective opinions and intended to be helpful to the particular readership at whom this book is aimed, but are not particularly authoritative.

The manuscript was typed by Yvonne Robinson. It was prepared for publication by Jean Finlayson, Publications Editor at the Further Education Staff College.

Acknowledgements

The Further Education Staff College is grateful for permission to include copyright material in this book from:

John Wiley and Sons for an extract from M. Klein, **Lives people live**, 1980. ISBN: 0-471-27649-9.

Prentice-Hall Inc., for an extract from S. Woollams and M. Brown, **TA: The total handbook of transactional analysis**, 1979. ISBN: 0-13-881912-2.

McGraw-Hill Book Company for an extract from R. Likert, **The human organisation: its management and value**, 1967. ISBN: 07-037851-7.

ABOUT THE AUTHOR

Dr. Colin M. Turner was born and bred in Birmingham. He took his first degree at Jesus College, Cambridge, and did postgraduate work at Leicester University. His degrees are in history.

Dr. Turner has taught in a variety of educational establishments. Since becoming a staff tutor at the Further Education Staff College he has been concerned in developing an approach to organisational behaviour which spans the disciplines of sociology, psychology and history. He has been active for the past 10 years in interpersonal skills training among educational staff and for industrial and commercial organisations. He has been much involved in transactional analysis, co-counselling and group training, and is currently working in a gestalt group.

Colin Turner lives in Wells, Somerset, where he pursues his interests in conservation and local history. He and his wife Jean have two daughters, both of whom are social workers.

Chapter 1

Introduction: The basic skills and assumptions

Life is built around relationships with other people. This is the source of much of our grief and much of our joy, it nurtures our creativity and development and fuels our destructiveness. The quality of our interpersonal relationships sets the quality of our lives. The skills we have and exercise in our interactions with other people, in our places of employment, in our homes and in our social activities are a critical part of our effectiveness as persons.

Very few people are likely to admit to others that they are bad at interpersonal skills any more than that they are incompetent at making love or driving a car. Yet we can all identify many around us who are clearly very bad at dealing with people, and another large group of our acquaintances, perhaps the majority, who are frequently inept. If so many of the people around us are clearly in need of improving their interpersonal skills, then perhaps that may also be their view of us. Self-honesty and a realisation of one's own lack of skill is a prior necessary state for investigation into the area of interpersonal skills.

There are broadly two distinct approaches to interpersonal skills training, each with a different set of assumptions.

1. The first concerns itself primarily with training in techniques of dealing with other people that will increase the likelihood that the objectives of the interaction are achieved. The assumption is that interpersonal techniques can be learnt in much the same way as the technique involved in skiing, wine-making or brick-laying. The purpose to which the skills are put are the business only of the user. He has a repertoire of techniques and will use whichever of them seem to answer the situation he is in. His assumptions may include a belief that he cannot trust people very far, that manipulation of other people is permissible if he can justify the purposes, that the effectiveness of his actions is compromised if his own weaknesses and fears are made manifest. The first approach will concentrate on the skills rather than on the person acquiring the skills. The assumption is that the skills can be separated from the person.

2. The second approach concerns itself first with the person, and only secondarily with the acquisition of skills. The fundamental basis of this approach is that until a person has explored and attended to himself — his fears and anxieties, repressions and phobias, rigidities and stresses — his relations with others will be contaminated and at the best will be less productive and at the worst will be destructive. The first move to go outwards to other people is to go inwards to the self.

It is the second approach which informs this book. If falls within the ambit of humanistic psychology and as such works on the following assumptions.

1

1. Man has the capacity for growth to high levels of creative, constructive and satisfying living.

2. People have within themselves the power to develop their potential, and therefore can take responsibility for that.

3. People are capable of choice. What a person is or does is what he has chosen. We are all therefore responsible for ourselves and our behaviour. We cannot use alibis or blame other people.

4. A person's growth is hindered if it involves damage to or manipulation of other people.

5. Growth is facilitated by a person's own self-awareness and understanding of his emotions, sensations, thoughts and perceptions.

6. Man is a whole, not a collection of parts. His mind, body and emotions can only function as an interrelated unity.

7. The humanistic psychology approach is therefore particularly concerned with:
   (a) encouraging those experiences which foster self-actualisation, spontaneity, loving, valuing authenticity, personal responsibility.
   (b) examining how organisations and social structures work and how they can be transformed into places in which people can flourish.
   (c) developing in people an understanding of their personal power so that they can take charge of their own life.

It is the basic tenet of this book that it is upon such assumptions that individuals can build competence in more technical skills of interpersonal relationships. Nine first-order skills are basic to all interactions.

BASIC SOCIAL SKILLS

Perceptual sensitivity
This is the ability to perceive more in other people's behaviour than is commonly the case. It requires firstly a high concentration on recording what is there — by listening much more carefully, observing much more thoroughly, and if it is relevant touching and smelling more fully. Most of us cannot listen to other people talking for very long without our minds wandering off.

Likewise we seldom look carefully at a person for very long to note what expression they have, how they are sitting, what body movements they are exhibiting. The habit of carefully recording what is going on so that we actually have a lot more information is something in which we can train ourselves.

The second stage is the developing of fine discrimination between the bits of information we get so that we can give them various meanings. This process of analysis of data involves the ability to interpret what different cues mean. In particular we learn what is implied by changes in facial expression, tone of voice, involuntary movements of feet and hands, posture and vocabulary. This also is something in which people can be trained.

Knowledge of self as seen by others

Most of us have very inaccurate images of how we are seen by others. We have some kind of self-image of what kind of person we think we are, and our assumption is that this is roughly how other people think of us. One of the more difficult skills is breaking through this type of thinking to the realisation that people have images and impressions of us of which we are unaware. Once we accept this we can begin to explore ways of discovering how we are typically seen by others. Note that this does not mean that we accept that other people are right or justified in the views they hold of us. The important thing is that if we are working with other people we are aware of the perceptions they have of use and can then work within this knowledge. Without it, our interactions with other people will be based on incomprehension. A part of the aim of most group training schemes is to confront a person with how he or she appears to other people in the group. Though this might be traumatic at first, it is an essential prelude to effective skill in interaction.

Taking the part of others

One of the abilities we have as human beings is the power to think ourselves into someone else's position and see life through their eyes. Clearly this is a useful social skill and is more highly-developed in some than others.

Giving recognition or strokes

People respond to compliments, rewards, recognition, praise, thanks, or, to use the generic term, strokes, and will modify their behaviour on the basis of the strokes they receive. Some people are very bad at giving strokes and this tends to make them disliked or distrusted. On the whole people who are popular and well liked give a lot of strokes to other people and do it sensitively and creatively. Clearly, if recognition reinforces behaviour, there is little joy to be had in reinforcing destructive or negative behaviour. On the other hand, only to give strokes for achieving well makes the process very conditional on performance. The skillful stroke-giver steers between these two extremes.

Feedback

Apart from learning how other people see us and developing sensitivity in interpreting the cues other people give us about our performance, we need to go further and modify our behaviour on the basis of this feedback. It is not enough simply to know: we also need to make use of the knowledge to improve our performance.

The independent performance of others

We have to work on the basis that our own behaviour has to fit in with that of other people. In social situations our capacity to influence someone else is not a one-way affair but is reactive and interactive, and each of us modifies our performance in the light of the other's performance. At a mechanical level, for example, we need to get a smooth synchronised sequence of speech and to do that each of us needs to adjust our pace and length of contribution to fit with the other. So there is a definable skill of synchronisation based on recognition of the independent activity of other people.

The presentation of self

We all present ourselves, in terms of our clothes, manner, conversation, etc., in accordance with the particular image of ourselves we want to display to others. This is sometimes called impression management, and it can be done with adroitness and skill or with ineptness. We do not expect the undertaker to tell jokes at a funeral, or the bank manager to be playing poker with his chief cashier when we go into his office. If we present the wrong or inappropriate image we are likely to cause embarrassment and a breakdown in interaction.

Recognising oneself

Finally, there is the most difficult skill of learning about ourselves and coming to terms with our own prejudices, fears, feelings and personality characteristics. When we feel good about ourselves on the basis of this kind of understanding, it enables us to feel not only confident in our own behaviour but to feel trust for other people and a respect for their own individual positions. This is a hard position to maintain all the time, but it is the basis of effective interaction with other people.

Giving trust

We are trusted as we trust. If we are suspicious of other people's motives and apprehensive of possible harmful actions against ourselves, then for certain we will create a like attitude towards ourselves. It is a self-reinforcing and self-fulfilling situation. Of course common sense dictates that there are times to keep our eyes open. Being trusting is not the same as being stupid, and those who accept dinner invitations from the Borgias need to eat with care. In nearly all cases we are likely to come across, however, it is simply a case of lact of trust breeding lack of trust, and if for no other reason it is a matter of practical convenience that interactions with other people are conducted in an atmosphere of reasonable trust. As suspicion generates suspicion, so trust will erode mistrust and encourage reciprocal trust. If that message seems too naive, it should be remembered that giving trust goes along with the other eight skills listed here. It does not stand on its own.

FURTHER READING

A useful introduction to social skills is given in:

ARGYLE, Michael **The psychology of interpersonal behaviour**. Harmondsworth, Penguin, 1970. ISBN 0-14-020853-4.

For those who like Argyle's approach, his ideas are developed at greater length in:

ARGYLE, Michael **Social interaction**. Tavistock, 1973. ISBN 0-422-75480-3.
ARGYLE, Michael **Social skills and work**. Methuen, 1981. ISBN 0-416-73010-8.

For those who want to explore the concepts of humanistic psychology, a good introduction is:

SHAFFER, John B. P. **Humanistic psychology**. Englewood-Cliffs., N.J., Prentice-Hall 1978. ISBN 0-13-447680-8 (pbk).

Alternatively information can be obtained from The Association for Humanistic Psychology in Britain, 62 Southwark Bridge Road, London SE1 0AS.

Chapter 2

Transactional analysis:
The basic concepts

INTRODUCTION

How can we as individuals try to make sense of the various relations or transactions we have with other people?

Most of us feel that we want to improve our skill in relating to other people and have many moments of feeling inadequate in a particular transaction. We might, for example, as Heads of Department be approached by a member of staff who wants to talk over some kind of problem, or we might get involved in a major row with the Principal. Outside our work life, we are likely to experience many more moments of clumsiness or inadequacy in transactions — with our adolescent sons and daughters, our spouses, our in-laws, our neighbours, our friends.

One of the difficulties of analysing and so improving our everyday behaviour with other people, is that the theories and writings of psychologists and social behaviourists have been very difficult for the layman to follow, both because of the language used and the complexity of the conceptual ideas. Read for example some Freudian or Gestalt theory.

The beauty of Transactional Analysis (or TA as we will now call it) is that its language is very simple, even colloquial — and, ironically, that in itself makes people very suspicious of it. We have been conditioned to expect to use long words to describe the way we relate to ourselves and other people. Not only is TA language simple, but its concepts are based on common sense, everyday observation of what we see and what we feel. There is very little underlying theory such as there is in Freudian psychology. The basic concepts of TA can be taught to anybody of average understanding in a few hours. It is true that, like all simple effective tools, TA concepts can be used to search deeper and deeper into human behaviour, but a useful level of understanding which can be put to practical use is available straight away.

There is nothing that can be said about the human condition that has not been said many times before over the last three millennia, and it would be wrong to make that claim for TA. Each age however has its own voice, and it was the particular gift of Eric Berne in his formulation of transactional analysis that he seemed to express the particular state of the late 20th century. It has proved a potent aid in individual and group therapy, in various forms of management training, and in all those professions which involve particularly close interpersonal relations — nursing, social work and teaching, for example.

TA is at one and the same time a method of analysing communications between people and a theory of psychological development. This dual function gives TA great flexibility and may account for the rapid spread of its use in recent years.

THE UNDERLYING ASSUMPTION

TA assumes that all the events and feelings that we have ever experienced are stored within us, as though on video-tape, and can be replayed. We can re-experience the events and, more importantly, we can re-experience the feelings of all our past years. Of particular significance, because they were so crowded with new feelings and experience, are the tapes from our childhood. We can relive the feelings we had of a child's joy or frustration, or our childhood perceptions of parental behaviour and commands. These feelings from our own childhood state and from our parents as experienced by us as children we carry around within us, and they are frequently reactivated. It is absolutely basic to TA, however, that all individuals have the capacity for change. Ultimately, the way we are is because that is the way we have chosen to be, and whatever the difficulties in so doing, we are free to make new choices. We are responsible for ourselves and cannot blame other people and other things for the way we are. The belief in the capacity for change makes TA a psychology of optimism. Eric Berne expressed this metaphorically by saying that everyone was born a prince or princess. Most people are persuaded that they have become frogs and so start behaving in a frog-like way. But it is in their power to stop waiting for the magic kiss, and instead choose to reaffirm that they are really princes or princesses.

OK – NOT-OK

We will start with one of the simplest of concepts: that of being OK or not-OK. The assumption is that we are always in one state or the other, and most people seem to spend much more time feeling not-OK than OK.

Being not-OK is experiencing discomfort, embarrassment, worry, apprehension, fear, boredom, lack of confidence, shyness, impotency and other such feelings. We may feel these more when we are on our own or more when we are with other people, but the likelihood is that during the average day we will have these discomforts nagging away below the surface. For much of the time they will be in a relatively mild form that we can well cope with, and we may regard them as just part of the human condition, but on occasions they will acquire quite dramatic forms. To check the truth of this argument, work forward from the time you got up this morning trying to identify the states of feeling you had minute by minute.

Being OK needs little explanation. It is the feeling of comfort, of being at ease, of feeling confident with oneself, and of joy with the world. It is experienced at moments of intimacy, of wonder, of total relaxation, of oneness with nature. We all feel OK sometimes, but it is not a continuous state and it may be only rare moments in the day when we feel truly OK. One of the purposes of TA is to move us more often from the not-OK states to an OK state.

When we are considering relationships with any other person at work or elsewhere, it is clear that we must not only be aware that we are operating from a not-OK state, but that the other person is likely to be doing so as well.

It might seem odd that we spend so much of our time feeling not-OK, but such seems to be the case, and furthermore we often develop various strategies and mechanisms to stay with and reinforce such feelings. If we are feeling depressed, for example, we tend to look for things or set up situations to make us further depressed rather than do the apparently obvious thing of looking for ways of feeling better.

RACKETS
We all at sometime experience all the following not-OK feelings.

Anger	Frustration	Stupidity	Fear
Guilt	Anxiety	Inadequacy	Clumsiness
Hurt	Loneliness	Rejection	Depression

One of these feelings however will be particularly familiar to each of us individually. It will have a special saliency. It is the one we know really well in all its shapes and contours and we have experienced the worst it can do. This is our racket, our favourite bad feeling. It is the feeling we will most commonly move into when we feel not-OK and its very familiarity gives us some comfort. So if we consider the varying reactions of a group of people to having a bump with another car, we would probably find one person straight away moving into anger, another feeling stupid, another feeling anxious about the other driver's reaction, another feeling guilt and so on. One stimulus will set off very different feelings in different people and it will happen in a patterned way. Likewise some feelings are very foreign to any individual. Just as he may be very familiar with guilt, he may hardly ever express anger and does not know very well what it feels like. Racket feelings are invariably inappropriate to the situation and must be clearly distinguished from genuine feelings clearly related to the external reality. It is, after all, very sensible to feel fear when an enraged bull is galloping towards you, but not when your boss is shouting at you. People will commonly set up situations to reinforce their rackets. Thus the Head of Department who has an anger racket will create situations several times a day when he can feel legitimately justified in being angry.

Rackets can be distinguished from genuine feelings by the fact that they are:

> Repetitive
> Inappropriate
> Manipulative

Rackets were learned in childhood. Whenever as a child we felt for various reasons not-OK, we had to find a behaviour which was accepted by the family and that was generally the racket modelled by parents. Thus, if during the bad times our parents tended to go off on their own and feel lonely and rejected, then that is probably what we learned to do. If they get angry, we will feel we have permission to be angry. And the more we get familiari with that feeling, the more we are likely to retreat to it.

EGO STATES
Fundamental to transactional analysis is the concept of ego states. If we look at the way people behave, we can observe them as appearing to exist in three separate discrete states, which we label the Parent, the Adult and the Child states. These states of behaviour seem associated with their own repertoire of vocal tones, gestures, expressions, attitudes and vocabulary which in turn seem to derive from different sources within ourselves.

To take an example: consider the staff member who comes bursting into a meeting with a broad grin on her face, and says, 'Hi, great to see you all again.' She sits down, looks towards the chairman and asks 'What is on the agenda today?' Then noticing the absence of one of the group, she says 'Don't say Bill is late again. It really is time he learnt to be on time.' Each of her three statements had its own set of expressions and gestures and seemed to come from different sources within her.

It was observation of these kinds of switches which led Berne into developing his theory of the three ego states. They are conventionally represented as shown in Diagram 1, page 8.

Diagram 1 — The three ego states

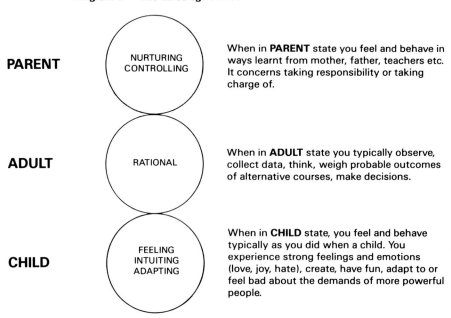

PARENT — NURTURING CONTROLLING

When in **PARENT** state you feel and behave in ways learnt from mother, father, teachers etc. It concerns taking responsibility or taking charge of.

ADULT — RATIONAL

When in **ADULT** state you typically observe, collect data, think, weigh probable outcomes of alternative courses, make decisions.

CHILD — FEELING INTUITING ADAPTING

When in **CHILD** state, you feel and behave typically as you did when a child. You experience strong feelings and emotions (love, joy, hate), create, have fun, adapt to or feel bad about the demands of more powerful people.

It is very important to understand that these ego states are not abstract concepts (such as Freud's ego, super ego and id) but actual states which can be observed. They can never be hypothesised, but must always be demonstrably present. Of course, one's vision might be defective so the behaviour might be misinterpreted, but this does not alter the fact that the behaviour is there.

How can we describe the three ego states?

The Child. In the first few months of our lives we experienced the world almost totally by feeling — feelings of satisfaction and contentment when we were fed, frustration and anger when we were hungry. As we grew, so we explored the world with curiosity, joy, pain and love. Experiencing the world through feeling is the hallmark of the Natural Child and it remains with us for the rest of our lives. Our joy at meeting a loved one, or our anger at being thwarted in our desires, is the same whether we are six or sixty. As the baby grows he begins to experience the pressure of the world of grown-ups about him. He finds he must adapt his

8

behaviour to please them rather than doing what he wants. Otherwise they cease to love him. He learns to be polite and submissive, and sometimes rebellious, and underneath he starts to learn about guilt and anxiety and other not-OK feelings. All the behaviour and feelings involved in adapting to other people we call the Adapted Child.

The toddler and youngster also learn to suss out what kinds of behaviour will get the responses he wants. He uses his intuition to guess that a smile to daddy will get him what he wants but it will not work with mummy. And as he gets older it is his Intuitive Child which enables him to 'feel' the right answer before he works it out logically. Artists and scientists rely heavily on their Intuitive Child for their most creative work. They work things out logically as well, but some of their most valuable work comes from the creative leap in the dark.

The Adult. When he is still very young the child begins to puzzle out things. He begins the process that he will continue all his life of taking in and processing information, and making informed judgements on that basis. This is his emerging Adult state. It has been referred to as the computer within us, and although this may give it a too limited role, it is an apt analogy. Whenever we are asking questions, giving answers, taking in or giving out information, assessing evidence rationally, judging between alternative actions based on likely outcomes, then we are in our Adult state. The Adult state goes through very rapid development between the ages of 6 and 12. It is a state which has little feeling in it. If we are experiencing strong feelings we cannot be in our Adult. This state has a capacity denied to the other two. It can view the activities of the Parent and Child, particularly if they are involved in some kind of tussle over what action you should take, and it can arbitrate between them. All of us who have experienced internal dialogues will be familiar with this process.

The Parent. As the young baby gets into childhood so she begins to incorporate from those older people around her feelings about what is right and wrong and how to help others. She begins to feel responsibility for other people, either by wanting to correct them or by helping them. Children at play can often be seen rehearsing these roles with their dolls or pets or younger siblings, by lecturing them on their misdeeds and by comforting them or bandaging them up. The Parent incorporates the moral and political codes, generally derived from mothers, fathers, school teachers and the like, and is concerned with what 'should be', what goals we ought to be aiming at. Its two aspects, therefore, are of the Critical Parent, which sets the rules and judges people against them, and of the Nurturing Parent, which cares for people. In a not-OK state the Parent is persecuting and prejudiced in its critical aspect. The not-OK side of nurturing is rescuing. In the TA world rescuing is not a good thing. It is defined as helping other people in order to help yourself feel better and to make the other person feel more helpless. It is really another form of persecution done under the guise of good deeds. Over-protection is a form of rescuing.

It takes relatively little practice to become proficient at diagnosing ego states because we are dealing with observable phenomena. We are looking for clues from the behaviour being engaged in, the vocabulary that is being used, the tone of voice, facial expression, gestures, postures and apparent attitude. Although we can most commonly listen to speech tone and content, it is easy enough to guess a person's ego state entirely from non-verbal clues. Imagine three people: one is standing very erect wagging his finger at a young child, his expression hard and stern. Another is standing in front of a machine pointing out to a workman he has with him the various operating devices. His expression is alert, his gestures active and decisive. A third is lying in the sun, absolutely relaxed, a smile of pleasure on his face. We do not need to know what is being said to be able to identify the three states of Parent, Adult and Child. Diagnostic chart 2 on page 11 does no more than suggest probabilities. It cannot be used conclusively to establish ego states, particularly when we are considering vocabulary. All the key words mentioned could be used in another ego state, though it would be less likely. All the clues when put together, however, should give a clear picture of the ego state being observed.

There are favourite arenas for ego states, though none is exclusive to one. We tend to be in our Child when we are in pubs, at sports matches, at the seaside, in bed. We tend to be in our Parent at church, at political meetings, when with our children (and perhaps too often in the classroom). We tend to be in our Adult in the lecture theatre, at our desk, or in the office.

What is useful for us in the concept of ego states?

It is a mark of a skilled and mature person that he or she can move easily between the states using whichever one is appropriate to the situation. It is important to understand that whatever the situation we face we have available to us responses from all the states. We can choose to respond from our Nurturing Parent, Critical Parent, Adult, Natural Child, Intuitive Child or Adaptive Child.

Let us consider an example: you are a head of department and your senior lecturer has been for an interview for promotion. You meet her coming back from it looking very downcast. She says:

> Well, that's another one I really messed up. What a shambles. I'm really mad at myself.

This clearly is a Child statement from a position of disappointment and frustration, very similar to the feelings we had as children in failing to come up to expectations or achieve well when we really wanted to.

You might make any of the following statements:

> Never mind, come into my office and tell me all about it (sympathetically).

> Well, you deserved it. I've always told you you ought to spend more time bothering about presentation.

> Are you willing to spend some time analysing where the interview seemed to go wrong?

> (nervously) Oh — er — well, I — er — don't know what to say really.

> To hell with them all — let's go and get drunk.

> Heh, I tell you what. Let's go and see Caroline.

It is the skill of the head of department to choose an approach that is appropriate for that person at that particular moment, and he needs to listen to his Intuitive Child for this. The likelihood, however, is that he, like the rest of us, is not able freely to move between the states and choose the most appropriate. That is

Diagram 2 – Indications of ego states

	CONTROLLING PARENT	NURTURING PARENT	ADULT	FREE CHILD	ADAPTED CHILD
BEHAVIOUR	Criticises Comands Dictates	Protects Comforts Helps	Equires Tests Reasons Gives and receives information	Cries Laughs Rages	Submits Accepts Rebels Reacts
ATTITUDE	Judgemental Moralistic Authoritarian	Understanding Caring Giving Smothering	Interested Observant Rational Evaluate	Curious Fun loving Changeable	Compliant Ashamed Apologetic Demanding
KEY WORDS	Must, Ought Always, Should, Wrong	Love, Good, Splendid, Well done, Help	How, What, Why, Consider, Probable	Super, Wow, Want, Fun, Ouch	Can't Try Sorry Thank you
VOICE TONE	Critical Condescending Sarcastic Firm Dominating	Loving Comforting Helpful Sugary	Calm, Clear Enquiring Precise Monotone	Free, Loud, Sexy, Energetic, Happy, Angry	Whiney Defiant Placating Moaning Demanding
GESTURES, POSTURES	Pointing finger Hands on hips Foot tapping Looking down on	Arm round shoulder Leaning Forward	Erect Pointing (to demonstrate)	Active Energy Cuddles	Slumped Pouting Cringing Foot stamping
EXPRESSION	Frowning Set jaw	Smiling Sympathetic Accepting	Alert Interested Pre-occupied	Uninhibited Laughter Excited	Dejected Apprehensive Pleading

because as we grow older we develop some ego states and diminish others. We have a favourite ego state and another which we seldom use. Maybe we find it easy to get into our Nurturing Parent on almost any excuse but do not use our Natural Child very often, or perhaps our Critical Parent and Adult are highly developed but our Nurturing Parent only makes the occasional appearance.

There is a useful device for examining this. It is called the egogram and was developed by one of Berne's colleagues, John Dusay. It requires you to consider your activities either in total or in particular aspects, such as at work or at home, over a stated period of time. This can be over a single day or several years. Of the aspects of ego states on the diagram, consider which you have been in most often and draw a bar to indicate that. Then consider which you have been in least and draw a bar to show that. Then consider in turn, and show appropriately, the next most common and the next least common states, and the surviving one in the middle. You could end up with something like Diagram 3 (below).

Diagram 3

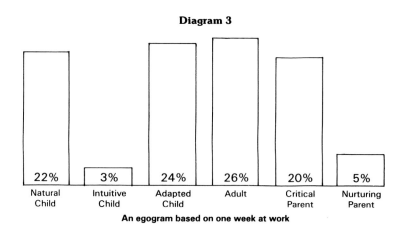

22%	3%	24%	26%	20%	5%
Natural Child	Intuitive Child	Adapted Child	Adult	Critical Parent	Nurturing Parent

An egogram based on one week at work

A lot that can be done in exploring egograms and Dusay explains this in his book. At the very least, however, we can look at our own egogram and ask ourselves whether this is how we want to be. There is no right and wrong. No one else has the right to say our pattern ought to be different. But if we feel we are too often in our Critical Parent and too seldom in our Natural Child, then we can set about changing that. There is a strong likelihodd that if we have a particular favourite ego state then that is the one we move into whenever we are under slight stress or face an unexpected situation. Thus the person whose egogram is shown in Diagram 3 would most likely use an Adult response to our senior lecturer who had failed to get his promotion.

One basic assumption behind TA, and indeed most other psychological and developmental theories, is that the amount of psychic energy we have is constant. We can redistribute it, use it in different ways, but we cannot increase or decrease it. What we are born with we have for life. So it is our choice how we distribute it round the ego states. If we increase one, we must decrease another.

For some people, their use of ego states gets totally out of balance. We probably all know:

The Constant Parents, who do little else but criticise others, advise others or take care of others — they seem to have no Adult or Child.

The Constant Adult, who continually analyses, lives only with facts, distrusts feelings; avoids moral and political questions, cares for no one.

The Constant Child who lives in his feelings all the time; consumed with anger, aggression or guilt, or always seeking fun or looking for kicks, or always feeling helpless, dependent or impotent.

The virtual absence of one or two ego states is referred to in TA terms as 'exclusion' and is a pathological state. For most of us it is a question of getting the balance right so that we can feel happy with our own lives and have the skill to relate sensitively to other people.

EGO STATES AND THE TRANSACTION

A transaction is a verbal exchange between two people (we will leave aside non-verbal transactions). One person speaks and the other responds. Transactions can be complementary and enable the conversation to continue, or they can be crossed and bring the conversation to an end or at least cause it to change its nature. To illustrate this let us consider the following simple transaction:

Head of Department (A): Have you seen that MSC file?
Secretary (B): It is in the central registry.

Here (A) spoke from his Adult to (B)'s Adult. This called for and received a reply from (B)'s Adult to (A)'s Adult. It was thus complementary and diagramatically would look like this:

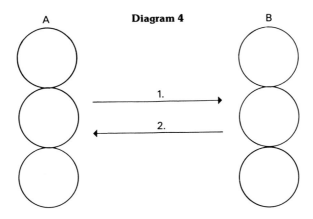

Diagram 4

Alternatively (A) might have said to (B)

Oh dear, I'm in awful trouble. You haven't seen the MSC report anywhere, have you?

to which (B) might have replied

Don't worry, I'll hunt it out for you and make sure nothing goes wrong.'

Here (A) spoke from his Adapted Child hoping for a protective Parent to come to his aid. (B) obliged, and so we have another complementary transaction:

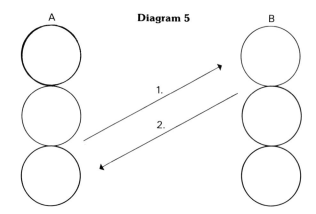

Diagram 5

A third alternative in the same situation is that (A) says to (B):

Where the hell is that damned file? I'm getting fed up to the teeth with this job.

And (B) might reply

Don't get at me. It's not my fault. I've got my own problems.

Here the Child state of the one is complemented well by the Child response of the other.

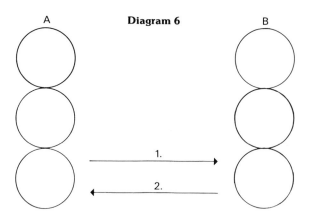

Diagram 6

All these are parallel transactions. The expected happens. There are no unusual responses and the conversations could carry on in that vein for quite a bit longer.

Suppose, however, that in response to the first Adult comment of the head of department:

Have you seen the MSC file?

(B) had replied, flustered and tearful,

Oh, don't say I've messed something else up.

Expecting an Adult response, the HoD is likely to be momentarily thrown by this emotional reaction from the secretary's Child. At this point (A) has choices.

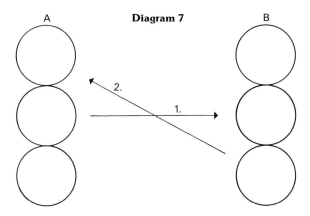

Diagram 7

(A) can carry on with Adult statements and try to pull (B) back to an Adult-Adult transaction. Or (A) can go into the Nurturing Parent role with a statement like:

There, there. Don't go getting upset. I'll go and find the file. You just forget all about it.

Alternatively (A) has the option of using the Critical Parent or Child roles. Whichever it is, the transaction has taken an unexpected line and is likely to land (A) in an undesirable position. If this happened once, it would not be of any concern but if it became a repetitive pattern and (A) was always being manipulated into the role of Nurturing Parent by (B), (A) ought to do something about it. After all, the pay-off for the secretary is that she does not have to be responsible and competent if she can always get someone to look after her.
So we need to be able to deal with crossed transactions when they happen to us. We also need to be able to make crosses when we want to switch the transactions we are in. For example, a particular type of Parent to Parent transaction is called the Blaming Parent, and it typically starts:

Isn't it awful what they are saying about the Principal?

and a typical response is:

Yes, I blame his secretary, you know.

If you do not want to join in this kind of transaction (which can go on for a very long time), then you can switch by an Adult response like

What is the evidence?

It is unlikely the initiator will really want an Adult-Adult conversation, and will most likely simply close the transaction.

To take another example, we can imagine a husband out at work all day and coming back into the home feeling tired and in need of comforting and coddling. His wife says, 'What kind of a day have you had?' He replies (pathetically) 'Oh, it's been a hell of a day. I'm really done in.'

She responds, 'Oh, never mind, put your feet up and I will bring you a cup of tea.'

He has come into the house in his Child looking for a Nurturing Parent and she has responded appropriately. But maybe she sometimes gets fed up with always nurturing the little boy in her husband and so decides to cross the transaction. When he says, 'Oh, I'm really tired. It's been a rough day,' she can give back an Adult-Adult response such as, 'Mrs. Smith came round today.' This throws him. He has to make a decision. Does he have another go at getting his wife to look after him. Does he switch into his Adult and say, 'Oh, did she? What did she want?' Does he decide his wife must be upset and go into his Nurturing Parent with, 'Are you feeling alright, love?' Does he feel angry at being ignored when he's been out earning the money all day and say from his Critical Parent, 'You might have a bit more sympathy. It's you I've been working all day to keep in luxury.' Whatever he does, the usual pattern has been broken.

ULTERIOR TRANSACTIONS

There is a form of transaction where behind the spoken message is a clear and unambiguous second message. This is shown diagramatically by a dotted line. The classic ulterior message is:

(A) Come up and see my etchings.
(B) That sounds a very interesting suggestion.

On the face of it this is an Adult-Adult transaction but we all recognise it as a Child-Child. It is always the ulterior message that has the power.

STROKING

All people from the moment they are born need the stimulation of stroking. Without it babies can actually die, and adults will shrivel up as personalities and occupy our mental hospitals. A stroke is a stimulation one person gives to another, and an exchange of strokes is one of the most important activities people engage in. Strokes are any act of recognition one person gives another. For babies and young children most strokes will be actual physical touching: with adults physical strokes are largely replaced by symbolic strokes such as praise or words of appreciation. Strokes can be either positive or negative — a kiss or a cuff. If the child cannot receive positive strokes from his friends or parents he will look for negative ones rather than get none at all. A blow is better than being totally ignored.

But it is the giving and receiving positive strokes that develops emotionally healthy people with a feeling of confidence in themselves, trust of others and a general feeling of being OK.

16

The kind of positive strokes that give this OK feeling, of everything being well with the world, must spread across the three ego states.

I require my Child to be stroked by being hugged.
I require my Adult to be stroked by being congratulated on my work.
I require my Parent to be stroked by being thanked for caring for someone.
I need to stroke other people's Child.
I need to stroke other people's Adult.
I need to stroke other people's Parent.

And all these strokes should be positive. We can diagramatically represent this in the following way:

Diagram 8

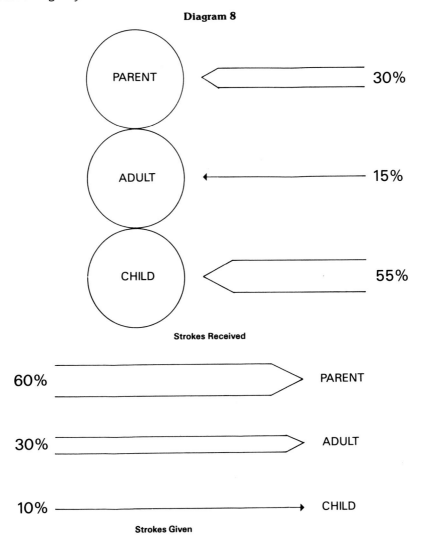

If we look at our stroking pattern in the way it relates to a person or group of people, we can make decisions about whether that is the way we want it to be, and change it if it is not. For example, we might find we are giving a secretary plenty of strokes but they are invariably for her Child ('You look marvellous today'), when what she might most value is some strokes for her Adult ('That's an excellent idea.') or for her Parent, ('Thank you for looking after those visitors.').

Another way of looking at our stroking pattern is by using the following device, shown in Diagram 9. It emphasises the difference between positive and negative strokes. We can complete it in relation to our work, our home or our social life. The patterns might be similar or different, the lack of positive strokes received at work being compensated to a point by plenty of strokes at home.

Diagram 9

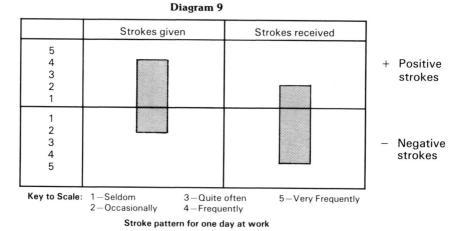

Key to Scale: 1—Seldom   3—Quite often   5—Very Frequently
2—Occasionally   4—Frequently

Stroke pattern for one day at work

The diagram shows the stroke pattern for a staff member who feels he gives more positive strokes than he gets back, and gives fewer negative strokes than he receives.

Our stroke pattern of giving and receiving will be very much conditioned by what kind of strokes we received as a baby and child. If we became used to negative strokes, to being smacked, criticised, shouted at, and generally put down, we will probably go through life looking for and giving negative strokes from and to other people. If we received positive strokes of praise, love and rewards, but only conditional upon performing well or conforming to the rules, then we will tend to give and look for strokes based on performance or acceptable behaviour. If we did not get much physical stroking, we will probably find it difficult to give such strokes.

One of our major difficulties is our inability to accept positive strokes. We have all sorts of ways of turning away or discounting the good things said to us. We have been taught the virtues of modesty and it comes hard to us simply to accept and take in a compliment. In theory it is easy enough. All we need do is say, 'Thank you. I appreciate that.' In fact we have enormous temptations to discount in some of the following ways:
1. Apply it to the giver:

18

You handled those students very well, Eric.
Oh, but not as well as you did.

2. Apply it elsewhere:

   Congratulations on getting your degree, Sonia.
   I owe it to my parents.

3. Globalise it:

   You have done a pretty good job on this project.
   Yes, the team did well. No one let the side down.

4. Don't see it (ignore it):

   That was a good speech — and your comment in question time was
   particularly valuable.

   Yes, it was a good speech.

5. Reject it:

   You did that very well.
   No, I didn't.

6. Discount the source:

   You look lovely today.
   You're bound to say that.

7. Unfavourable interpretation:

   That's a lovely dress you're wearing today.
   Didn't you like the one I wore yesterday?

8. Analyse it:

   Why do you think he said that to me?

Although there may be good reasons why you do not want to accept a stroke, and
you certainly do not have to, it is worth remembering that a discounted stroke is a
slap in the face for the giver. That may not be what the discounter intends, but that
is how it comes out.

Strokes are very potent. One of the most powerful ways to use TA to change
your own life is to look at your own stroke pattern and then change it by giving
more positive unconditional strokes at work and outside work. The effect on
colleagues, employees, wives, friends will always be beneficial to them and to
you.

LIFE POSITIONS

The experiences of the baby and child during his first few years, particularly the
strokes or lack of strokes, and the prescriptions and proscriptions he receives from
parents, teachers and other adults, lead him to take basic positions about himself.
These decisions become generalised into the basic OK and no-OK psychological
positions. There are four of these positions:

19

The OK Corral

I'M OK YOU'RE NOT OK	I'M OK YOU'RE OK
I'M NOT OK YOU'RE NOT OK	I'M NOT OK YOU'RE OK

The child who comes to accept his own worth and that of other people, who can trust other people and feel confidence in himself, is in an I'm OK, you're OK position. Very few people seem to be able to operate in this position, but it is the most constructive, creative and healthy, and enables openness and intimacy to exist between people.

For most of us our early experience were of being put down, criticised, made to feel a fool, made to feel powerless or inadequate by parents, teachers, big brothers, etc. and we incorporate enough feelings about our own various inadequacies to carry though these feelings into our adult life and work from the position I'm not-OK, you're OK. If we think about our nervousness before making a speech or facing an argument with our boss, or our embarrassment when our colleague behaves strangely in public, or our apprehension when waiting for comments on our performance, we see the not-OK feelings of our Child within us. We can probably guess that about three-quarters of all people are generally in this position.

A few people have such a brutalised experience, physically or psychologically, in their childhood, that for their own survival they switch positions to I'm OK, you're not OK, and as they take this into adulthood they are likely to display signs of megalomania, dictatorial or persecuting behaviour. At its strongest level it produced Hitler; at a more moderate level principals or parents who are forever getting angry with and putting down their subordinates or children. The I'm not OK, you're not OK position is one of black despair in which few people can be for very long without damaging their personality. It is the world of depressives and suicides.

Although we can move temporarily into another position, we are most of the time bound by the one which we were led to accept early in our life. Skilled therapy can certainly move people into more healthy positions, however, and TA therapists have had considerable successes in this.

TIME

Everyone of us has the existential problem of what to do with the next few minutes or hours. For everyone of us time sometimes drags and sometimes races by, but one way or another we have to fill it. We have a limited range of choices. Berne suggested that we can pass time in one of the following ways:

1. **Withdrawal.** We can go into ourselves, detached from other people, and daydream, fantasise or meditate. If we are sitting on a train just watching the scenery go by, or in a lecture room thinking back to some enjoyable experiences the night before, we are structuring our time by withdrawal.

2. **Rituals.** We can pass the time by highly stylised exchanges with other people, where there is a minimum of content but interchanges of mutual

recognition between people. It is typified by the greetings exchange:

Hi!
Hello there!
How's things?
Fine, how about you?
Fine. Be seeing you then.
Sure. Cheers.
Cheerio.

3. **Activities.** This is what we might normally call work. Giving a lecture, replacing a window, cleaning the car, operating the computer are all activities and may or may not involve us with other people.

4. **Pastimes** are ways of passing the time by pleasant cocktail party chat on safe subjects which require little thought and where responses are automatic. They have a somewhat repetitive quality and often start with a statement such as, 'What car are you driving now?', 'How's the baby getting along?', 'What recipe did you use for this cake?' They are, in Berne's words 'largely socially programmed by talking about acceptable subjects in acceptable ways'.

5. **Games** are sets of ulterior transactions with well-defined psychological gains and losses. These are discussed in the next section.

6. Finally, there is **Intimacy**, an open relationship of mutual free giving and receiving without exploitation. It is the most exciting, deep, rewarding, but for some people the most frightening, of the ways of passing time.

The six ways of time structuring are produced here in ascending order of risk. The total openness of intimacy involves risk, the total closedness of withdrawal gives almost total safety. We all pattern our time differently. There are people who spend much time in withdrawal and ritual, and when they do get more closely involved with people have to do it by games playing. Other people spend most of their time in Activities and Pastimes. There are some mature and fortunate people who can spend quite considerable time in intimacy. An examination of your own time structuring over a week will enable you to decide whether you want to make changes or not.

GAMES

It was Eric Berne's analysis of psychological games in his best-seller **Games People Play** (1964) that first brought TA to the attention of the public. This was unfortunate in a way because a great deal of superficial interest in games developed without much serious thought as to what lay behind them, nor equivalent interest in the other areas of TA.

Games are transactions between people which are always destructive to at least one of the players and leave behind feelings of not being OK. They are compulsive and repetitive. People play the same games over and over again. Why do people engage in them?

Games provide for those taking part in them a number of 'rewards'. They satisfy our rackets — that is, they enable us to feel justified in feeling angry, stupid, incompetent or whatever our racket is.

They reinforce our particular life position.

They provide us with a lot of strokes of the kind we want — and for some games players these are negative strokes.

They pass the time and thus avoid the need to spend it more constructively (e.g. in intimacy or withdrawal) but more threateningly.

They have a pay-off in terms of some existential problem the player has.

Game playing is explained most easily by taking two or three examples.

GAME 1

A lecturer comes into the Head of Department's office, looking worried.

> Lecturer (A): 'I wonder if you can help me? I've got a real problem.'
> H.o.D. (B): 'Of course. Just sit yourself down and tell me all about it.'
> (A): 'I've been teaching for six months now and I am still making a mess of it. I'm just not making it as a teacher.'
> (B): 'Why don't you apply for one of the inservice courses for teachers at Garnett College?'
> (A): 'I'd love that, but my wife's pregnant and I don't want to be away from her more than I have to be the next four months.'
> (B): 'Well, how about the evening sessions the Professional Tutor is organising on teaching methods?'
> (A): 'Most evenings are really tricky for me just at the moment.'
> (B): 'You could read some of the books on teaching. They might help.'
> (A): 'Yes, but I don't learn easily from reading things in books.'
> (B): 'Why don't you go and talk to Jim? He's a very skilful teacher, and I'm sure he would be willing to help you.'
> (A): 'I've thought of that, but what works for him, wouldn't work for me.'
> (B): 'Well . . . why don't you take a tape recorder into the classroom. You could play it back and find out where you were going wrong.'
> (A): 'I don't think I'd be at ease with a machine going.'

At this point the Head of Department runs out of ideas. B can do one of two things but neither of them will do any good because she/he is well and truly hooked.

1ST VARIATION

> (B): 'I don't know. I can't really think of anything else. I'm sorry.'
> (A): 'Well, I guessed you wouldn't be willing to help me.'

The HoD feels a sense of failure and criticism from the lecturer so he/she feels bad. The lecturer feels that if he doesn't get any help when he asks for it, it's not surprising he isn't teaching well, so he goes away confirmed in his racket of incompetence. He can carry on being bad and not have the responsibility of trying to get better.

2ND VARIATION

> (B): (angrily) 'Look, I keep on making suggestions and all you do is dismiss them. You've got to get a grip of yourself or you'll never make a teacher.'
> (A): 'There you are, you see. I come to get help and all anyone can do is get angry with me. How can you expect me to get better?'

22

The lecturer goes away feeling justified in his incompetence. He has manoeuvred the HoD to appear to be unsympathetic to his problem, and the Head is left feeling bad.

This game is known as 'Why don't you — yet but', and is very common in organisations. The following are the points to notice about it.

1. The lecturer starts by hooking the Nurturing Parent of the Head of Department. If he cannot do that, the game won't work so he will only play this with someone with a strong Nurturing Parent. Games always require two players, and the initiator of the game looks round for the susceptible person. Once found, the game will be played over and over again in various forms.

2. There is a stage in every game when there is a cross over. Roles change and the knife goes in. In this case it occurs when the Head runs out of ideas and is likely to move either to Adapted Child or Critical Parent. This is what the lecturer is waiting for. He quickly moves into Critical Parent and leaves the scene.

3. The lecturer goes away not only feeling legitimated in his failure but also with an important pay-off — that he need take no responsibility for his performance. The most common kinds of pay-offs in games are: avoiding responsibility for your actions, avoiding intimacy, or avoiding the consequences of one's work (copping out).

4. The game was very stroke-rich. The lecturer got a lot of attention and concern which filled a need he had for strokes.

5. The way to avoid being dragged more than once into this game (almost everyone falls for it first time round) is to keep a firm check on your Nurturing Parent and respond to the initial hook by an Adult statement like:

    'Could you come back tomorrow at 10.00 with some ideas of what methods you might find useful, and we can discuss them.'

The Head will not be bothered with this games player again. The last thing the lecturer wants is a solution.

GAME 2

A course team leader comes into the Vice Principal's office.

Vice Principal (A): 'We have to have this course submission ready very quickly. Sorry about it but the committee have been on to me. What's the earliest you can get it done by?

Team leader (B): 'If we cut all the corners and I work over the weekends I can let you have it in two weeks.'

(A): 'Two weeks! Far too long. I cannot wait that long. I must have it in seven days. If not, believe me, some heads will roll.'

The team work very hard on the submission but still haven't finished after seven days. The Vice Principal then sends for them and demands angrily to know why they haven't finished and goes on to describe a whole series of faults, failings and unsatisfactory characteristics the incompetent and lazy team leader has, and discusses him with a whole series of undefined threats.

23

This is a simple version of the game known as NIGYSOB (Now I've got you son of a bitch'). It consists of setting a person up to knock them down, in this case by giving an impossible task and then attacking someone for failing at it. It can equally well be set up by giving ambiguous instructions, conflicting instructions or changing the rules half way through. The pay-off for the Vice Principal is that he can legitimately satisfy his anger racket, and he can feel that failures are not his fault but those of his incompetent underlings. He can only play this with someone, however, who is prepared to take an Adapted Child role and who requires to be kicked in order to satisfy his racket. So he can go away feeling hurt, a failure, guilty or whatever his particular racket is. This is a complementary game in that a NIGYSOB player is looking for a Kick Me player, and when the two meet, they will cherish each other. The last person the NIGYSOB boss would ever want to sack is his Kick Me subordinate. The game is easily broken at the point where the Vice Principal's unreasonable time limit is given. A response could be:

'I'm sorry. I cannot do it in seven days and you will have to accept that. I will finish it in 14 days but no sooner.'

Whatever the Vice Principal's response, he will realise he hasn't got a player for NIGYSOB.

GAME 3

This is a game which normally takes place over a period of time, though it can refer to the activities of one day. A lecturer has made a very favourable impression since he was appointed a few months ago. He has worked very hard, often late into the evening and has several schemes in various stages of completion for improving the range and quality of the department's work. One of his colleagues goes sick for several weeks and he takes over her classes. He sits on several committees and has never yet turned down any request by the Principal that he involves himself in some new body. He is also in the middle of working for his M.Sc. via a thesis on management. When one of the Vice Principals goes ill, he volunteers to take over some of her planning work. Everyone sees him as a dynamic, hard-working man for whom future promotion is inevitable, though a number wonder how ever he does it all.

Then just before his schemes come to completion, his thesis is written and his job application goes in for a Vice Principal's job, he collapses. Over-work, the doctor says, and orders him six months rest. He was a great chap, worked like fury, say his colleagues as they pick up the bits and pieces of his schemes and course submissions, committee memberships and the like. No one criticises him, everyone regards him highly. And yet what he has set up is a game, the purpose of which is to enable him legitimately to cop out, to fail to deliver or achieve what he is supposed to achieve. He is a person frightened of the responsibility of having to be accountable for his work, and so makes sure he never quite completes the projects. In the process he gets a very large number of strokes and can legitimately feel he is a highly competent person who would have achieved great things if only it had not been for his breakdown in health.

This is a common game among business executives, some of whom work quite hard to get their heart attack. It can be played in a small way over selected projects, such as the running of a conference or over the whole of one's work. It is a difficult one to deal with, but if it is recognised early enough colleagues can refuse to allow that level of over-work in so far as they have that power. This game is a version of 'Harried', and cop out or accountability-avoiding games are found in several manifestations.

GAME 4
The final in this short selection of games is taken from a social situation and the reader is asked to transfer it to a situation between two colleagues at work. Two partners, Ann and James, are sitting at home one evening. Ann initiates the game by a series of non-verbal sighs, grimaces, pouts and chain-smoking.

James 'What the hell's the matter with you tonight?'
Ann 'None of your business.'
James 'If you're in one of your stupid moods, I'm clearing out off to the pub.'

When he returns some hours later he faces angry recriminations but gives as good as he gets.

Ann 'What time do you call this? You're in a disgusting state.'
James 'Don't you shout at me! If you make it worth staying at home I would. You drive a man to drink.'
Ann 'If you can't see what was worrying me you're more insensitive than I thought.'
James 'You've been unbearable ever since your mother came to stay last month, the stupid cow.'
Ann 'Don't you talk about my mother like that. What about your mother . . . and so on.
At some stage one or the other storms out slamming the door, and makes for the spare bedroom.

This is a game, appropriately called Uproar, which requires both to be in Angry Child leading into Critical Parent leading back to Angry Child. If either goes into Nurturing Parent or Adapted Child in its submissive form, it will not work. Although it looks a straight row, it is in fact a contrived game which is played repetitively and there is no danger of the two people splitting up. They need each other. Their problem is that they want to live together but find it difficult handling intimacy. Therefore they have to set up situations which enable them to get apart from each other.

Like all games it passes time in a way relatively safe to them, and it is very stroke rich, initially via negative strokes, but full of good strokes when they make up the following morning.

There are many other variations of games and the reader is referred to the standard texts including Eric Berne's **Games People Play**.

PRACTICAL APPLICATIONS OF TA IN THE COLLEGE
We can apply TA to our working life in the college. Most obviously we can examine our own typical work transactions and see if they satisfy us as being flexible and appropriate to the situations we are in. Are we too often operating from our Parent or our Adult? We can examine our stroke pattern and see if we

give as many strokes as we think we do, and whether our strokes are appropriate and freely given or conditional in some way. Are we set in certain stroke patterns where we always stroke the Child of our secretary and the Adult of our teaching staff? The rethinking of our stroke pattern is probably the most powerful single activity for change that we can undertake. Likewise we need to look at how we receive strokes: do we accept them or reject them? What difference will it make to our relationship with the givers if we start accepting strokes we have previously rejected?

With knowledge of our rackets, what kinds of games are we playing with those in charge of us and those we are responsible for? Are we initiating games or merely being hooked into them by those around us? How are we going to break out of our games?

With practice we can begin to apply TA to our interactions with other people, developing more flexibility and social control and reducing the amount of manipulation and the feeling of being not-OK.

If we look at our organisations as a whole, we can describe our college, department or section in TA terms:

It is very Parental — if so does this come out in nurturing, rule-setting, or controlling?

Does our organisation cope with the need to express the Free Child — is it sometimes a Fun organisation?

Is our organisation strokey or non-strokey? If it does seem to encourage a lot of strokes, are they positive or negative, conditional or unconditional?

Is our organisation in the position of I'm OK — You're OK? If not, what?

Whatever the situation, the important point is that we as individuals have the power to begin to change.

FURTHER READING

It is important that the first book you read gives a comprehensive explanation of TA.

Introductory Books

JAMES, Muriel and Jongeward, Dorothy **Born to win: transactional analysis with Gestalt experiments**. N.Y. Signet Books, 1978. ISBN 0-451-08169-2.
This book contains many exercises with which the reader might not wish to be bothered, but the text itself forms a very clear introduction to TA.

JAMES, Muriel and Jongeward, Dorothy **Winning with people: group exercises in transactional analysis**. Addison-Wesley, 1973. ISBN 0-201-03314-3.
A companion book to the above and itself serves as a good simple introduction, but the value of this book is in its exercises, intended to be done in groups but easily adapted to individual use.

HARRIS, Thomas A. **I'm OK: you're OK**. Pan, 1973. ISBN 0-330-23543-5.
Another best-seller and the first six chapters are very readable. Most TA theorists would now challenge Harris' understanding of some of the key concepts. Read with care.

WOOLLAMS, S. and Brown T. A. **The total handbook of transactional analysis**. Englewood Cliffs, N.J., Prentice-Hall, 1979. ISBN 0-13-881912-2.
A very good introduction, which assumes slightly more of the reader than some of the other books.

KLEIN, M. **Lives people live**. Wiley, 1980. ISBN 0-471-27649-9.
A bit more than an introduction. It relates TA to psychoanalytic thought, deals with some pathologies in TA terms, and gives examples of therapy sessions.

STEINER, C. **Scripts people live**. N.Y., Grove Press, 1974. ISBN 0-394-49267-6.
This is an excellent book which is centred on scripts.

STEINER, C. **Games alcoholics play**. N.Y., Grove Press, 1971. ISBN 0-345-28470-4.
This is a short, well-written and very penetrating book on scripts but particularly concerned with self-destructive behaviour and its accompanying set of games.

DUSAY, J. **Egograms**. Bantam, 1980. ISBN 0-553-11850-1.
A very good exploration of the egogram as a technique for self-examination.

MCKENNA, Jim **I feel more like I do now than when I first came in**. St. Louis, Formur, 1975.
Don't try to understand the title, ignore the appalling sub-editing, and stagger through the bad writing. It has a lot to say about stroke profiles and makes some useful unorthodox points on the way.

BIRNBAUM, J. **How to stop hating and start loving**. Pan, 1977. ISBN 0-330-24064-7.
A popularisation of TA theory that is easy to read and with good examples. Its particular value is its concentration on hostility and anger.

TANNER, Ira J. **Loneliness: the fear of love**. Harper & Rowe, 1973. ISBN 0-00601-4218-9.

Though this is not such an easy book, it is short. It assumes familiarity with TA language and thingking. Its value is in its analysis of loneliness and feelings of being unloved.

Books on Management

BARKER, David **Transactional analysis and training**. Gower, 1980. ISBN 0-566-02118-8.
The best of the books in this section and written by an English person for a change. (Mavis Klein is also English). It is written from the point of view of a management trainer.

MENINGER, Jut **Success through transactional analysis**. N.Y., Signet, 1973.
It's approach may be brash and the style unpleasant and the examples are all taken from American business life, but it has some useful points to make.

BENNETT, Dudley **Transactional analysis and the manager**. American Management Association, 1979. ISBN 0-8144-7511-6.
Another book aimed at American business people and written in a plain 'no nonsense' style, but usefully focuses on the manager's job.

JONGEWARD, Dorothy *et al.* **Everybody wins: transactional analysis applied to organisations**. Addison-Wesley, rev. ed., 1976. ISBN 0-201-03271-6.
Contains some useful detailed examples of the application of TA to business and industrial firms. The contributions vary in interest and quality.

JAMES, Muriel **The OK boss**. Bantam, 1975. ISBN 0-203-03272-4.
Another from this prolific stable and useful enough.

TA and Radicalism

TA has generally been seen as a therapeutic or adjusting approach to people who are at odds with the world. A more radically political line has been developed by a group of psychotherapists on the West Coast of the USA under the general inspiration of Claude Steiner.

STEINER, C. ed. **Readings in radical psychiatry**. N.Y., Grove Press, 1975. ISBN 0-394-17868-6.
Read particularly the manifesto and the chapters on principles, alienation and the stroke economy.

WYCOFF, H. ed. **Love, therapy and politics**. N.Y., Grove Press, 1976. ISBN 0-394-17906-4.
A further collection of essays in the same vein.

TA and Feminism

The above two books are informed with a general feminist view and there are a number of specific chapters on women. Read particularly Hogie Wycoff's chapter on Women's Scripts and the Stroke Economy and Problem Solving Groups for Women by the same author reproduced in both Stenier and Wycoff.

JONGEWARD, Dorothy and Scott, D. **Women as winners: transactional analysis for personal growth**. Addison-Wesley, 1976. ISBN 0-201-03435-2 (pbk).
This covers some basic TA theory, but then analyses women's role in TA terms. Liberal rather than radical.

The Berne Collection

Sooner or later one has to approach Berne's books — later rather than sooner because they are not easy. Berne writes in an elusive, allusive, humourous, elliptical and metaphorical style which make him easy to misunderstand and his crucial insights are easy to miss on a first reading. There is a danger of hero-worshipping him. Not all his books are particularly good. The following are certainly worth study.

BERNE, Eric **What do say after you say hello?** Corgi, 1975. ISBN 0-552-09806-X.

At his most brilliant and the culmination of his life's thinking. If you only read one of his books, this is it.

BERNE, Eric **Games people play**. N.Y., Grove Press, 1964.

A best-seller in its day, but generally misunderstood, and it needs to be read in the context of his other works.

Finally

Two books not classified elsewhere:

BARNES, Graham ed. **Transactional analysis after Eric Berne: teachings and practices of three TA schools**. N.Y. Harpers College Press, 1977. ISBN 0-061-68412-0.

A textbook with various authors exploring the current state of TA theory. Fine if you like heavy-going theory.

REDDY, M. **Handbook for TA users**. The Author, 1980.

An excellent book, in loose-leaf form with 56 sheets on various aspects of TA divided into general background material, theory, applications, exercises and training materials, and review and research material.

Available from the author, 90 Church Road, Woburn Sands, Bucks.

There are now considerable numbers of books on TA in the bookshops. Many are not worth reading, but there will be some of real worth which do not appear on this list. After becoming familiar with one or two of the main texts, however, the reader will be able to make his own judgement of what is worthwhile and what is a rip-off.

If you have difficulty in purchasing these books, they are generally available at:

Compendium Bookshop, 240 Camden High Street, LONDON.
Prometheus Bookshop, 134 Alcester Road, BIRMINGHAM.
Changes Bookshop, 8 St. Michaels Hill, BRISTOL.

It should be noted that most of these books use the phrase 'Little Professor' where I have used 'Intuitive Child'.

Chapter 3

Transactional analysis: miniscripts and drivers

The idea of miniscripts was first put forward in an article by Taibi Kahler and Hedges Capers in the **Transactional Analysis Journal** (Jan. 1974). Kahler developed the concept in a chapter in Graham Barnes (Ed.), **Transactional Analysis After Eric Berne**, in 1977. There has been growing interest in this country in the last few years, particularly through the advocacy of Mavis Klein who has used miniscript in her psycho-therapy practice and has written about it in **Lives People Live** (1980). Miniscript is concerned with repetitive behaviours which are accompanied by not-OK feelings, that we live through over short periods of time — minutes or even seconds. It is an attempt to discover at that basic level the causes, the dynamic, and the consequences of our behaviour.

In early childhood, we are frequently faced with worrying, frightening or confusing situations which are caused by the adults about us, and which we do not understand. There is not much that we can do to change this directly, because we are so powerless in a world of powerful people. We experience various kinds and intensities of bad feelings, and look for ways of getting out of those feelings, so that we can feel good again.

One way of doing this is to work out that if we do certain kinds of things or behave in certain ways, we are likely to be looked on more favourably and receive strokes and approval. Our Little Professor works out what it is that seems likely to achieve that particular effect in our family. There are, so it is claimed by Kahler, only five of these conditional approvals.

> I will be OK if I am perfect
> I will be OK if I am strong
> I will be OK if I please you
> I will be OK if I try hard
> I will be OK if I hurry up

These are known as the five **Drivers**. Almost everyone of us develops one particularly strong driver, with perhaps another relatively strong subsidiary one.

We move into behaviour which is associated with our Driver because we hope by that means to get rid of our bad feelings, but in fact the relief is bound to be very short-lived. People will approve of us if we can achieve our designated goal, but we are always unsuccessful. Failure is written into the operation. If being approved of is conditional on being perfect, being strong, etc., we are never going to achieve it for very long, if at all.

As we experience the impossibility of reaching or maintaining the behaviour we have set ourselves, we have a number of choices of where we can move. We may move back to where we started and wait for events round us to change and so for our feelings to change. There are however another three possible stages in the miniscript; one might go through one or two or all three of them.

The first of these is called the **Stopper**, which is another word for a Racket. When we realise that our attempts to show ourselves as perfect do not get the approval which we need, either from ourselves or other people, we move into whatever habitual bad feeling we tend to seek when things are not going well for us, and with which we have at least the comfort of familiarity. There is no automatic association of a particular Stopper with a particular Driver, but there will be a commonsense relationship. We might find, for example, individuals who had the following Drives and Stoppers.

Be Perfect   — Feeling guilty
Hurry Up   — Panic
Try Hard   — Fear of failure
Please Others — Feeling embarrassed
Be Strong   — Feeling unappreciated

It should be emphasised however that a completely different set of Stoppers could be equally appropriate.

Another stage in the miniscript is that of the Vengeful Child. This is a reversal or a rebellion against the demands of the Driver, and again is an attempt to gain some feeling of OKness, however temporary and fragile. In this case the individual has to get rid of his bad feeling of not living up to his Driver by pushing the blame on to someone else.

The fourth stage is that of the Final Pay-off. If what we are really seeking is some very hard confirmation of what we really think of ourselves in relation to our lives, then we may move into that bleak position. The movement through the miniscript can follow three courses on its route between the Driver and the Final Pay-off, and can at any stage break out of the miniscript and return to pre-Driver behaviour. The customary way of diagramming it is shown in Diagram 1.

Diagram 1

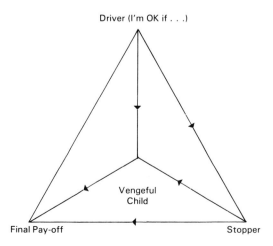

31

An alternative diagram is as follows:

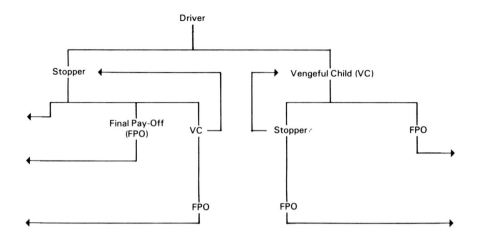

Diagram 2 — Table of the Miniscript Cycle

Driver	Typical Stopper	Typical V.C.	Typical F.P.O.
Be perfect	Guilt	Makes a total mess of things	Worthlessness Depression
Be strong	Unappreciated	Invulnerable to others. Boredom	Cannot get close. Not worthy of love
Please me	Misunderstood Embarrassed	Wilfully lacks consideration for others. Rudeness	Inauthenticity. No one lets me be myself
Try hard	Fear of failure	I could be the best if I bothered	I'm not as good as I think
Hurry up	Panic. Can't think. Tiredness	Lateness Immobility	Not belonging Craziness

The way in which the miniscript works, very often just over a few seconds of time, can best be illustrated by examples.

First example: A man with a very strong Hurry Up driver is on a bus to the railway station. He is going for an interview and is anxious to do well as he has failed in his last three applications for jobs. He has therefore rushed his breakfast, dashed out of his house to catch a bus, and sprinted to get on one just leaving the stop. If the bus takes its usual time, he will arrive at the station 45 minutes before his train goes, but he is worried about unexpected events. He sits down on his seat breathless but feeling relieved that everything should be allright now. However, as the bus stops and starts along its journey he becomes more and more worried and impatient with each traffic light, with each long queue at a bus stop, with every slow moving vehicle. Finally the bus gets stuck in traffic at a road works and he experiences extreme anxiety bordering on panic that he will miss the train (Stopper). As he waits there, he says in his mind to his wife, 'It's all your fault. I wanted to go up overnight. It was you who said there was plenty of time in the

32

morning. It will serve you right if I don't get it — I don't want to go through with the damned interview anyway.' (Vengeful Child). As he thinks of his lost chances, however, he becomes more and more dispirited, and a feeling of what a failure in life he is gradually pervades him (Final Pay-off). At that point a dog nearly runs under a bicycle and his attention is switched to that. That particular cycle of the miniscript is over. In fact he arrives at the station with 30 minutes to wait, and stamps about the platform impatiently, wondering why he always ends up having to wait for trains.

Second example: A housewife believes that she has to have everything done perfectly for her family — the house absolutely clean and tidy, the meals properly cooked and seved, etc. (Driver). As she becomes totally exhausted after a hard morning of clearing up and preparing for her families wants and needs, she begins to feel being used unfairly by others who take her hard work for granted (Stopper). She goes to bed and lies down all afternoon, letting everything go to pieces. The meal wasn't prepared, the washing was half completed and the vacuum was in the middle of the sitting room (Vengeful Child). As her family returns, she comes down and surveys the mess. She thinks 'I'm no good at looking after my family. I'm a failure' (Final Pay-off).

Third Example: This example is taken from my own behaviour. If the miniscript works it ought to work for me, and I have found many instances where I have spotted my Driver behaviour in operation. I was running a conference and a visiting speaker set up an exercise which led her to divide the groups into threes. From my Be Strong driver, I immediately thought I needed to take charge and make sure no groups of two or one were left over. I had feelings of not having coped properly (Stopper). Then I thought 'I don't care. Let them sort the mess out themselves', and went off with another two members to the point furthest away from the activity I could find (Vengeful Child). I did not actually get into a Final Pay-off.

Kahler and Klein produce tables and lists of various kinds of behavioural signs that indicate Driver behaviour.

Diagram 3 — Key Diagnostic Clues

	Miniscript	Words	Body Language
1.	Be Perfect	Perfect, Worthless, Clean, Dirty, Tidy, Untidy, Should, Shouldn't, Obviously, As it were, Believe, Of course, Depression, Exactly, Actually, Precisely, It's not my fault, For my sins.	Precision, over-qualification won't be interrupted, Itemizing and numbering of points while talking, purses bottom lip between forefinger and thumb.
2.	Be Strong	Strong, Weak, Boring, Pull yourself together, I don't care, No comment, Vulnerable, It's no good getting upset, You don't appreciate what I'm saying.	Over-straight back, legs crossed, has moustache, pulls socks up.
3.	Please Me	Dear, Really?, Nice, Pleasant, Bastard, Y'know I mean, Please yourself, Embarrassed, Super, You misunderstand me.	Nods head, raised eyebrows, looks away, (men) runs fingers through hair, horizontal lines on forehead, questioning inflexion.
4.	Try Hard	Try, Could, Couldn't, Impossible, Superior, Inferior, Fail, Succeed I don't know, It's hard, Lucky, Unlucky, I'm better than, Not as good as you/him/her.	Sitting forward, elbows on legs, chin in hand, puzzled look, asks more than one question at a time, does not answer question asked, stutters.
5.	Hurry Up	Hurry up, Panic, Anxiety, Quickly, Energy, Tired, Crazy time, It's pointless, It's futile.	Brows knitted into vertical lines between the eyes, speaks rapidly and interrupts himself and others, fidgety, breathless, eyes shiftly.

From the book, **Lives People Live** by Mavis Klein. Published by J. Wiley and Sons Ltd. © 1980.

Diagram 4 – Driver Chart: One Person's Driver Behaviour

Driver	Physical Sensation	Internal Discount	Words	Tones	Gestures	Postures	Facial Expressions
Be Perfect	Tense, robotlike	'You should do better'	'of course' 'obviously' 'efficacious' 'clearly' 'I think' (tells more than asked)	Clipped righteous	Counting on fingers, cocked wrist, scratching hand	Erect, rigid	Stern, ashamed, embarrassed
Try Hard	Tight stomach, tense shoulders	'You've got to try' 'I'll try' 'I don't know' (doesn't answer questions—repeats, tangents)	'It's hard' 'I can't'	Impatient	Clenched, moving fists	Sitting forward, elbows on legs	Slight frown, perplexed look
Please Me (Someone)	Tight stomach	'You're not good enough'; 'Make others feel good'	'You know' 'Could you' 'Can you' 'Kinda' 'Um Hmm' 'Would you'	High whine	Hands out-stretched, head nodding frequently	Head nodding	Raised eye-brows, looks away
Hurry Up	Antsy	'You'll never get it done'	'Let's go' (interrupts people—finishes their sentences)	Up and down	Squirms, taps fingers	Moves quickly	Frowning, eyes shifting rapidly
Be Strong	Numb, rigid	'You can't let them know you're weak'	'No comment' 'I don't care' (doesn't use here-and-now feelings)	Hard, monotone	Hands rigid, arms folded	Rigid, one leg over	Plastic, hard, cold

From the book **TA: The Total Handbook of Transactional Analysis** by Stan Woollams and Michael Brown © 1979.
Published by Prentice-Hall, Inc. Englewood Cliffs, NJ 07632

34

It is likely that we all at various times experience each of these five driver behavioural patterns, but it is the belief of Kahler and Klein that our primary driver can be diagnosed by careful attention to the clues they provide in the above tables. Klein makes it clear that these are not hypothesised *a priori* but were developed out of empirical observation in her practice of psychotherapy. In Kahler's table, the first two columns of Driver-related activity are not observable by any one other than the subject. Only she can know what physical sensations she is experiencing, and what internal discount is drumming away in her brain. The remaining five columns contain information which can be observed by an outsider — a counsellor, friend or psychotherapist.

The miniscript as a concept is still in evolution, and the following criticisms are intended to help sharpen up the concept rather than to deny its usefulness. The major weakness is in the named Drivers. At the moment there are five, but there is no reason to suppose this will not in time be extended. There is nothing immutable about five. However, given that at the moment we consider the five named by Kahler, we can raise questions about the diverse kinds of behaviour each is apparently covering. For a label to be of use, all the parts covered must have sufficient in common to make it possible to use the label as convenient shorthand in general discussion or analysis, and if we refer back to any one of its parts this should not cause confusion or ambiguity. I am uncertain whether the labels given by Kahler satisfy this criterion, and some of the difficulties I find in using the miniscript relate to the source of this uncertainty. Put simply, I think a label such as Be Strong covers too many different meanings. We can illustrate this and help tidy up the concept of miniscript by considering each of the Drivers in turn.

Be Strong. Behaviour in this Driver can derive from a number of quite different sources.

(a) A Be Strong person can be driven by the feeling that he is tough enough to handle anything that comes along. There is nothing that will find him out or break him down.

(b) A second person can be driven by the feeling that he is above such weaknesses as emotions. He is the tough impassive person, hard as a rock, and apparently without feelings.

(c) Another person is driven to take charge of or assume responsibility for everything that is going on around him. He is strong enough to look after everyone and everything.

(d) Another kind of Be Strong person is driven by the need to be totally independent. He believes he can deal with everything on his own and does not need other people. In fact he is uncomfortable if dependent on others.

(e) A further kind of person is driven by the need to be in total control both of himself and of other people.

There are no doubt other Be Strong variants as well, but the number given here makes the point that this Driver applied to one person simply does not mean the same thing as the same Driver applied to another. Clearly there are some obvious similarities between the types, but there are also major differences which will result in quite different kinds of behaviour. This is why I suspect the utility of the tables of diagnostic signs given by Kahler and Klein. If we were to make some general remarks about Be Strong people, we might say that they tend to avoid physical and verbal intimacy, they are not open or trusting, and they avoid vulnerable situations at all costs. They make a virtue out of pain, suffering, discomfort and overwork, assuming it is good for the soul and strengthens the character. They have great concern over control, particularly of their own feelings, and are often taciturn. It is likely they have received strong messages of 'don't be a child', 'don't have fun', and 'don't feel'. They probably have strong feelings of rejections and find close intimacy difficult, probably because their parents were never close to them, either physically or emotionally. They are often committed rescuers. In their bad moments they tend to feel unappreciated in spite of all the strength they give to others. A final pay-off feeling is very often extreme feelings of loneliness and rejection.

The problem with such a series of defining statements is that they apply much more to some variants of Be Strong than others, and not at all in some cases. The person who takes responsibility all the time, for example, may be vulnerable, talkative and with good intimate relations with many people.

Be Perfect. Woollams has suggested that this can be of many types, some of which he defines as follows:

(a) The person who is driven by the need to be absolutely clear and precise in everything he does, with no possible room for ambiguity. Her normal conversation sounds like a civil service letter, e.g. 'I will give careful consideration to the points you have just raised, and when it is clear to me which course of action will lead to the best results . . .'

(b) The person who tries to cover every possibility so that nothing is left in doubt. 'On the one hand you can take this view, at least if you can establish that any of the following alternatives are viable, though if one of them is not correct you will be in error, unless you are correct in spite of an erroneous assumption because of other factors. On the other hand . . .'

(c) The person who describes exactly what is happening with no comment or interpretation. Such a person never uses metaphors nor makes qualitative judgements or speculations.

(d) The person who keeps quiet, because if he says or does something he might be wrong. He will not risk making a mistake.

(e) The person who judges others by picking up the errors and illogicalities in what they say, often on trivial points. He will not let anything pass without putting it through a rigorous critical test.

(f) The person who judges rather like a chair person of an arbitration panel. She waits until everyone has spoken their piece, then delivers her judgement in measured and certain voice. It may or may not be approving, but it will always be patronising.

The Be Perfect person uses long words and sentences, and enjoys debate and dispute on almost any issue, however small. He will introduce a lot of qualifications, and will commonly comment on or redefine a question rather than answer it. They will often look complacent, or sometimes impatient at other people's imperfections. Klein suggest, without giving her evidence, that it is common among people with Jewish or Roman Catholic backgrounds. It is often focussed on sexual behaviour. Obsessive or compulsive behaviour is common, for example, in following precise rituals, being obsessively tidy or clean, not stepping on the lines in pavements, etc. There is often a Child message of 'Grow up', 'Don't be a child'. Depression is often associated with the Be Perfect Driver.

Again we can argue that these behaviours do not fit all the types of Woollams' list. For example, the Be Perfect by Being Exact does not enjoy debate and dispute, and tends to use short sentences with short and simple words. The Be Perfect by taking no risks also does not enjoy debate and will avoid making judgements at all costs.

Hurry Up. Generally there is rather less written about this Driver than the other four. It is said to be typified by people who cannot keep still, talk hurriedly and frequently interrupt others, always seem to be in a rush, and are inclined to panic. The injunctions from childhood seem to be 'Don't think', and there is a tendency towards hysteria sometimes resulting in a total inability to do anything at all. Generally Hurry Up people make a mess of things.

There are two significant points to make about the Hurry Up Driver. Firstly, it is important to know whether a person is hurrying away from, or hurrying towards, or just hurrying aimlessly, as his typical Driver behaviour. One Hurry Up person will always be anxious to be away from where he is, checking his watch almost from the moment he comes in. Another person is always anxious about where he has got to be in half an hour's time, and can never settle to where he is because of this worry about the future. A third person just hurries about anxiously as a compulsive behaviour.

The second and more crucial point is that we need to know whether the Hurry Up person typically messes things up and loses out, or whether he does get where he is going and achieves what he wants. In this latter case he will always arrive much too early for the train or the party but he will at least be there. His Driver forces him into compulsive behaviour about getting there, but apart from wasting time, he will get through his day without mishap. In the former case he will rush so much that he forgets his ticket, leaves the door unlocked, trips over a kerbstone, runs and catches the wrong bus and fails to make the train or the party. The behaviours of these two kinds of people are different, the pay-offs are different, the games are different, the injunctions are different, and it does not help to merge them together under one label. In most TA books, reference is only made to the loser Hurry Up Driver hurrying towards something and with the injunction to mess things up. This is far too limited a focus.

Try Hard. The compulsive behaviour of trying hard at whatever you are doing and the feeling that most people will see you as OK if you are clearly working hard is a common enough phenomenon, particularly in Anglo-Saxon non-conformist cultures. The assumption of most of the TA books however is that the Try Hard person is the perpetual loser, the one who never makes it, and that is the essence of the Driver. While it is true that the Try Hard person gets his drive and justification from trying and not from achieving, that does not mean that he does not achieve. I believe that many people with a very strong Try Hard Driver do normally achieve what they try hard at, but the achievement gives them only a limited satisfaction, and they immediately look around for something fresh to try hard at, so that they can fill up the time and feel relatively good. Messages as a child were of the kind, 'You can only do your best', 'If at first you don't succeed', etc., and their school reports no doubt most commonly said, 'tries hard', or 'works hard'. Try Hard people compare themselves with other people or their own past performance on all sorts of dimensions. They think in terms of league tables and mark lists and are always competing with an outside standard. The English educational system is very good at reinforcing Try Hard Drivers. In discussion on this Driver two concepts are intermingled and often confused — Try Hard and Work Hard. There is a benefit in separating them out as two separate Drivers, or at least be aware that they mean somewhat different things.

Please Me. Of the five Drivers, this is the most unambiguous. It derives from a heavily over-adaptive Child state, with parental injunctions not to pay attention to and value one's own needs and feelings. They are conditioned to feel good when helping other people to feel good. It is the position of the arch-rescuer and is built around the myths of duty, self-denial, self-sacrifice and saintliness. The underlying parental message is 'don't be you', part of the script is 'don't leave me', and the typical internal discount is 'what I want (need, think) doesn't matter'. The two main variants of Please Me are the strong rescuer and the weak doormat. The strong rescuer is very positive in her statements about sacrificing her own needs to other people, and expects recognition and reward for this, and plays her games and seeks for pay-offs from that position of strength. One can visualise it as a combination of Please Me and Be Strong. The doormat is anxious, apologetic, guilty and underneath probably resentful. He can be visualised as combining Please Me with Try Hard or Hurry Up, and his games are likely to be played from a Kick Me victim position.

This brief analysis of the five driver positions throws some doubt on the use of the labels unless on each occasion some further qualification is made. This is not generally done in the literature and leads to some ambiguity and confusion. Some people may prefer to keep to the five Drivers but discipline themselves not to use them as shorthand labels. I would tentatively suggest that it would be worth experimenting with the use of two further Drivers — Be Responsible For, and Work Hard. It may or may not turn out to be of help in the analysis of miniscript behaviour, but experimenting with the concept of Drivers is a necessary and creative activity for the advance of our understanding.

FURTHER READING IN MINISCRIPTS

KAHLER, T. and Capers H. The miniscript. **Transactional Analysis Journal** Vol. 4 No. 2 1974.

This was the basic text and was developed in the following work.

KAHLER, T. The miniscript.
in: BARNES, G. ed. **Transactional analysis after Eric Berne**. N.Y., Harper College Press, 1977. ISBN 0-061-68412-0.

KLEIN, M. **Lives people live**. Wiley 1980. ISBN 0-471-27649-9.

This devotes a chapter to the miniscript and has dispensed with much of the scholasticism of Kahler. It rather over-generalises but has a useful section on dealing with your driver and on the dynamic of combinations of drivers. Ms. Klein has been working on love and friendship relations in miniscripts, i.e. how the couples with different drivers relate to each other. She is shortly to publish a book on her findings.

WOOLLAMS, Stan and Brown, Michael. **TA: The total handbook of transactional analysis**. Englewood-Cliffs, N.J., Prentice-Hall, 1979. ISBN 0-138-81912-2 (pbk).

This has a brief but clear summary of miniscript theory in the chapter 'The Script in Action'. It is useful as a first introduction to the miniscript.

Chapter 4

Transactional analysis: Scripts

WHAT IS A SCRIPT?

Our script conditions our lives. It is the basis on which we live out our days. It determines much of our behaviour, our images of ourselves and others, our dreams, ambitions and expectations. Our script is formed when we are very young. It is in the process of making from our birth up to the age of seven or eight. After that, though we may modify it in various ways, its main lines are set. We have by then come to some firm decisions about what we are like, what others are like, what life is all about, and what part we are going to play in it. Henceforth we are captive to our script, and dutifully play out our role. To reach greater freedom and autonomy we have first to understand what our script is, and secondly to move out of script behaviour as often as we can.

How is a script formed in the first place? We need to try to imagine ourselves back into our very early years — say when we were two. We have to think how small we are in a world full of big people, big furniture, big voices. In this world we constantly face all sorts of unpredictable and random events. We face quite unexpectedly the full force of the bad feelings and the good feelings of other people. It is a confusing, frightening world and we have to try to make sense of it in order to want to carry on with life at all. We want to find out what the rules are, what seems to work most of the time, what is expected of us, what life is all about.

We are at that age, however, very vulnerable indeed. This is so in four particular ways:

1. We are very weak and powerless. Almost everyone is much stronger than we are.

2. We are not, at that age, able to deal with or tolerate high levels of anxiety or stress.

3. We have only a rudimentary thinking capacity. Rational or logical thought is undeveloped and wrong conclusions are easily drawn.

4. We lack information at this age. Our total sum of data is very restricted and very focussed. Most information comes to us via our custodians, often in heavily screened form. In particular, we do not have sufficient information to compare the behaviour we see in our home with knowledge about what goes on in the rest of the world.

The child normally has no option about where she lives, and whom she lives with, but in the vulnerable state she is in has nevertheless to get by and make sense of what is happening around her.

The process of making sense of the world, of coming to decisions about it and her place in it, is what is meant by forming a script.

How does she do this? Primarily by listening to the thousands of messages she receives about herself and others, and the world in which they live, and then trying to fit them all together. Not everything she hears will be worked into her script. Messages she hears will vary in frequency. If her mother says just once to her in exasperation, 'You are so stupid', it will probably not be a significant part of the script. However if the child hears in some form or other messages about her stupidity every day, then it will be an important part of her script. The potency of a message also depends on its source. The comments of a mother living in the home are likely to be much more significant than those of a neighbour or the big boy living down the road. Messages are also given with different emotional intensity, and it is the ones with a heavy emotional charge that are likely to make the most impact.

MECHANISMS FOR LEARNING SCRIPTS

There are three particular ways in which the child picks up messages about her-self. These categories are not discrete, and many messages will spread across them, but they illustrate the particular mechanisms at work.

Modelling

The child has various behaviours modelled for her by the significant adults in her life. The behaviours often give clear and consistent messages. For example, she might see a father who works very hard and takes little time for his own enjoyment. She might well draw a message from this that being a man is a serious business; his role in life is to work hard and support his family. She might see her mother give way to her father in every argument, and so decide women shouldn't stand up for themselves. Modelling is particularly concerned with sex scripting, but also affects all other scripting such as adult-child modelling — which says, this is what an adult is, and this is what a child is.

Attributing

Each child must hear several times a day comments which describe him or attribute qualities to him. Anything that defines or labels the child in some way can be included in this category, e.g. 'You're bad, stupid, idle, careless, clumsy, thoughtless. You're just like your father. You'll never be as bright as your brother. You're not pretty but you're cute. You're a lad! A pity you're not strong like the others'. When these messages are heard day after day, and receive particular force through the circumstances when they are said or the intensity with which they are said, the child almost inevitably has to come to a decision to believe he is like that — bad, or stupid, or clumsy, or a drag like his father, etc. The messages do not of course have to be verbal. A father might give presents to his daughter, which always reinforce the message, 'You're physically attractive', and never that 'You're intelligent'.

Suggesting

Adults can give to children clear indications of what they want or expect. For example, a child hearing frequently a statement 'don't bother me', might decide it is better to keep away from people unless he has been particularly good. A state-ment, 'don't hang around me all the time', might lead to a decision. 'I've got to make it on my own — they won't help me'. A statement, 'nobody cares about me'

41

by a mother might lead a son to decide, 'I must give up my own needs, and stay around to look after her'.

MESSAGE TYPES

It is common sense that not all messages are harmful. Many are essential for survival in the world without hurt, others are the basis of developing or growing in autonomy and creativity. Messages such as 'be yourself', 'believe in yourself', 'enjoy the world', 'give and receive love', are all the kind of messages called **permissions**. They permit or allow the child to develop naturally, without artificially implanted limitations. He has maximum free choice and a chance to fulfil his potential. A child who receives plenty of permission messages will also be given a great deal of unconditional stroking. Indeed the unconditional stroke is the most powerful message to be yourself and value yourself. To separate these kinds of useful nurturing, caring and freeing messages, from script messages, Shulamit Peck refers to the first as the person's story and the second as the person's script. The former is allowing, the latter is limiting.

Script messages are most commonly in the form of injunctions or prescriptions. In whatever form they are expressed, they are likely to concern one of a very small number of crucial and basic messages that the child has to come to terms with. The following are the major crucial messages which can be given to the child either as permissions or injunctions with various degrees of qualification.

Permission: Exist.   Injunction: Don't exist

The basic message the child receives from the moment she is born is whether her parents want her around. If she is given strokes and acceptance, and valued for being there, then she will want to live and belong, and she will develop a sense of trust and optimism. If she is ignored, not handled or stroked as a baby, kept out of the way, she will only have a tentative drive to live, and feel her life is not worth anything.

This message is often transposed into:

Permission: Be healthy and strong.   Injunction: Be weak. Die.

A child can receive messages that she is weakly, susceptible to illness, likely to catch everything that is going around. The unstated message probably is, 'You are going to die' (I want you to die). If this is incorporated into script decisions, such people who have a potential for a healthy life no different to anyone else, will grow up plagued with illness and an ever-present concern about ill-health. Many of her activities will help her achieve an ill-health script through bad eating habits, smoking, avoidance of elementary health precautions, restricted breathing, etc. Most children are given permission to grow up healthy and strong and set about doing that.

Permission: Feel and express   Injunction: Don't feel.
emotions.

If children are allowed freely to laugh, cry, feel anger, frustration and fear without scripty messages, they grow up feeling comfortable in having and expressing a wide range of emotions. If such expressions of feeling are supressed by parents in childhood, children learn to discount and distrust their emotions and feelings.

42

Such messages as 'boys don't cry', 'of course you're not frightened', 'don't shout so much', will cause such discount. Instead of genuine and appropriate feelings, children learn to substitute the feelings their parents are prepared to approve of or at least live with. Such substitute feelings are **racket feelings**.

Permission: Have and be aware of   Injunction: Don't feel sensations.
physical sensations.

Children will naturally learn to use all their senses — visual, kinesthetic, auditory, olfactory, gustatory. Children may not receive permission to acknowledge sensations fully. Instead the messages they receive may be not to feel hunger or pain, not to see ('don't stare', 'concentrate on what you are doing'), etc. Such a person grows up detached and split off from her body and its sensations.

Permission: Think.   Injunction: Don't think.

The child needs permission and encouragement to think for himself, to develop his Adult ego state. Parents who encourage and value their child's ideas, questions, interests, enthusiasms, curiosity, creativity, allow the child to feel it is OK to think for himself. If his attempts to think are discounted by ignoring, making fun of, or putting down, then the child will grow up with a clear message that it is not a good thing to think for himself and trust his mind.

Permission: Be close to others.   Injunction: Don't be close.
Don't belong.

The growing child needs messages, particularly non-verbal and by modelling, that it is OK to be physically and emotionally close to others. If the child is not cuddled and stroked, if parents are remote to him and each other, then he may grow up with an injunction to keep distant from people. He will experience difficulty in belonging. This injunction can be caused by the departure or death of a parent, when the child learns that it doesn't pay to get too close, because in the end you only get hurt or let down.

Permission: Be who you are.   Injunction: Don't be you.

The child needs confirming messages that her physical appearance as it develops is accepted by her parents. Every child learns quickly which sex she is and whether it is approved of by her parents. Her messages may be that boys are more valuable, or a boy may learn that he is the wrong sex because his mother wanted a girl. Approval of criticism of shape (You're growing fat like your father), of height (all the rest of your brothers are tall), colour, hair, eyes, legs, etc. are given in hundreds of messages to children. Discounting messages lead to a script with a powerful injunction against being as you are.

Permission: Be your age.   Injunction: Hurry and grow up, or
Don't grow up.

Messages given to a child may be to grow up quickly because parents are unhappy with young children, or want to be on their own, or don't want the financial burden. In such cases the child gets a message that it is not OK to be a child, to be needy and dependent on others, and finds it difficult to be carefree and playful. Conversely parents may not want their children to grow up because they feel good when they have someone to look after and be dependent on them, or because they fear what nasty things will happen to their child when it goes through and beyond puberty. A child may get both messages — don't be a child needing our care and energy, but don't grow up and be independent and leave home. The script message is a very powerful one to stay at home and take care of the parents. Children need permission to be and enjoy the age they are, and also to go back to behaviours from previous ages on occasion. All ages anyone has lived through are good ages.

Permission: Succeed.   Injunction: Don't make it.

To give a child strong messages to succeed can be done in many ways — by encouragement, attribution, modelling, etc. Conversely, parents who put limitations and obstacles in a child's way, who feel jealous towards her, or pass on their own incapacity to work for their own success, will limit their child's capacity to develop an inner sense of competency. He will feel afraid or guilty doing well at something. Some messages of this type relate to siblings — for example, not letting a younger brother go to grammer school because the elder failed, or not letting a daughter stay in the sixth form because the son was an academic failure. It is very difficult to have permission to succeed if the child has been given any of the previous eight injunctions — e.g. succeed but don't think, don't be close to others, don't exist, etc.

WHERE DO THE MESSAGES COME FROM?
Messages are not given by parents with carefully calculated malice nor randomly. They are given out of the parents' own scripts. It is useful to distinguish the individual scripts of parents from those they carry by virtue of their position or status, and we will look at the latter first.

Ethnic or Cultural Script Messages
A good many messages are given to children because they belong within a given ethnic or cultural group. The parent is the transmitter on behalf of his or her ethno-cultural group. Many messages relate to being Jewish, Welsh, Afro-Asian, Australian, Sikh, Geordie, Baptist, etc. Many of these messages will relate to national identity, age scripting, sex role, religious belief and observance, and stereotyping of other ethnic/cultural groups.

Socio-Economic Class Script Messages
Many messages are related to socio-economic class, and help establish for the child class identification and behaviour. These are often related to manners of dress and speech, and also to political orientation.

Family Messages
Some families have a very strong family script, which all the members over the years try to pass on to their children. Typical script messages are:

'Our family is always in trouble with the police'.
'We've looked after the village for generations'.
'We've always had one black sheep in the family'.
'No-one tells a Blackwood what to do'.
'We've never asked for help from anyone'.

44

Often, a parent will pass on the family saga or myth:

'We've been working our way up in the world for generations'.
'Grandad was a foundling — but he made a fortune'.
'We used to be gentry once'.

Very often related to this, though it might more properly come under the next section, is the vocational message. Many children get very strong messages about what they should become, either generally, e.g. 'You go to university and get on in the world', or specifically, e.g. 'We've always been doctors in this family', or 'You'll make a splendid parson', or 'You be a docker like your Dad'.

Individual Parents' Messages

The majority of messages, however, are those that are consistently given, week after week, year after year, by the grown-ups in our lives. Some of these messages are good. They come from the OK part of their Parent, Adult and Child, and help make the growing child a good Nurturing Parent, with a confident and clear-thinking Adult, a fun-loving Free Child, and an Adaptive Child that is flexible enough to encourage good relationships and ease of living. Many of the messages are bad. They come from the not-OK part of our parents, and are a part of the script they were given when they were young. This script resides in their Adaptive Child but might come out in the form of apparent Parental injunctions and pre-scriptions. It is commonly called the Pig Parent, and the growing child is almost totally defenceless against it, while the grown-up may not even be aware of the way in which he is off-loading his own script and not-OKness into his daughter or son. In many of the TA textbooks, script matrices are drawn to demonstrate how the messages are passed on. The following matrix, illustrated by two messages, applies to a child aged two or three.

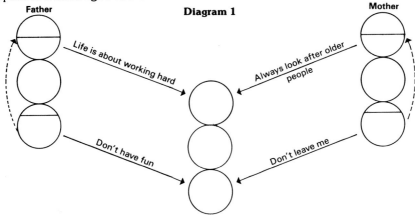

Diagram 1

Father — Life is about working hard — Don't have fun

Mother — Always look after older people — Don't leave me

Child aged 2-3

As the child grows older, he develops a stronger Adult which is not dependent upon other people defining his thinking and reality for him, and an independent Parent which works out what are the rules and responsibilities he wants to live by. The script messages from childhood stay as tapes, however, and are firmly embedded in the Child ego state, though they will often come out as Parental statements. At the age of 18, the script matrix will have changed thus.

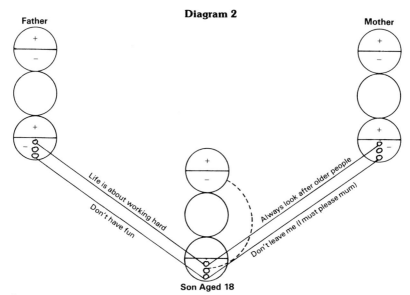

Diagram 2

Father

Mother

Life is about working hard

Don't have fun

Always look after older people

Don't leave me (I must please mum)

Son Aged 18

The messages from the father's and mother's own not-OK child are now locked into the not-OK Child of their grown-up son and will emerge as tapes from his past either in his Child or not-OK Parent.

The messages which have been useful, liberating, and allowing will have come from his father's and mother's OK ego states and will have helped their son form his mature Parent and Adult state.

HOW TO FIND OUT ABOUT YOUR SCRIPT

Script analysis, whether done by yourself or another, is simply a process of finding out and getting into some kind of order the script messages you have received and are bound by. There is no standard process. Some TA workers prefer using a questionnaire, others prefer using occasional stimulus questions and free association to see what comes up. It is useful to work with another person, changing roles halfway through the session. If you do this, the person working on his script must take prime responsibility for the activity: the other person is there as a facilitator, asking questions and making suggestions but does not carry the responsibility for solving the other person's script identification.

At the start it is useful to collect together all that you have learned about yourself from working through the other parts of TA. To start working back to your script messages you need to address yourself to such questions as the following:

1. What do you remember or have been told about your grandparents?
2. What kind of person was your mother — and your father?
3. What was the story of your birth? Who told you about it?
4. Why were you called by your forename(s)?
5. What was/is your nickname?
6. When you think of your mother in your childhood what is she doing? — and what is she saying to you?

46

7. When you think of your father in your childhood what is he doing? — and what is he saying to you?
8. What did your parents want you to become?
9. Think of when you felt really good with your father.
10. Think of when you felt really bad with your father.
11. Think of when you felt really good with your mother.
12. Think of when you felt really bad with your mother.
13. What was your favourite fairy story or child story?
14. Who was your favourite hero (male or female)?
15. How old do you expect to be when you die?
16. What will you die of?
17. What will be written on your tombstone? — and on the back?
18. Write down all the things you remember your parents passing on to you?

This last question needs some time given to it. Many of the things you remember will probably be parental advice or commands — e.g. keep your shoes clean, wash your hands, you can only do your best, look after your mother, don't interrupt, etc. Aim for about 30 items.

Lists of script questions can be found in many TA text books, but it is important to treat them simply as stimulus questions. You should not feel obliged to find an answer, nor keep your answer to the limits of the question asked. If you have no response to a question, then leave it. If, for example, you have no memories of any comments about your birth, then pass on to the next question, though do not be surprised if much later you suddenly remember a birth story that had got deeply buried in your memory. Allow answers to the questions to lead where they will go by free association. You may find that three or four of these questions set off hours of remembered material which makes the remaining questions superfluous.

As you work through this material, the key elements in your script will start coming through loud and clear. You do not need to be a clever therapist to do this. All you need is persistence, commonsense, a determination to be honest with yourself, and confidence in your ability to understand yourself better than anyone else can (though as said before it is beneficial to do it as a mutual activity with a peer). As tentative conclusions are formed about script messages, check them out with yourself and other people. If they feel right to you, then they almost certainly are right. During script analysis, it is important to be aware of the significance of the signs your body and speech will give — changes in breathing, a particular emotional charge on a specific word in a sentence. Nobody ever picks up all the clues, but most people with concentration and effort can pick up enough to discover the script messages that lie underneath.

PATTERNS OF SCRIPT
Many people's scripts fall more or less into overall patterns over the life span. There are six major patterns which are commonly postulated.

The Never Script
This script binds a person never to get what he wants. He may talk about or start all sorts of projects, and he may try awfully hard, but he will never actually achieve

what he wants — he never gets married, never becomes a doctor, never goes to America, never enjoys sex, never writes his book — in fact whatever he sets himself up to do, his script behaviour will make sure he fails to achieve.

The Always Script

This is the converse. A person with this script always feel constrained to carry on doing the same as she is doing now. Such a person may always stay at home looking after other people; always work in the same depressing job; always move about from place to place or whatever particular role she has committed herself to performing for life.

The Until (Before) Script

This script binds a person to defer his reward until certain other activities have been completed. Everything is conditional upon first accomplishing the appropriate labour. He might live a life full of self-denial and hard work to enjoy life in the hereafter; or work hard while the children are young to enjoy life and have fun when they are off his hands.

The After Script

Someone living out an 'after' script assumes that everything she now has that she enjoys, she will have to pay for in the future. If she has good health, illness will catch up with her later. If she is born into wealth, she will be made destitute some time in the future. She can never accept what she has now, without thinking what is to come after.

Almost (Over and Over) Script

The 'almost' script binds a person almost to achieve what he wants, but always to fail at the final hurdle. He repeats over and over again his efforts to get there and every time just fails. Such people almost get their degree, almost clinch the sale, almost break the record, almost buy a house.

The Open-Ended Script

The open-ended script leaves a person with no direction after a certain part of her life is over. She is given a script to marry and bring up children, but no instruction of what to do when they are grown up. So she loses any orientation and purpose in life when that happens. She may be scripted to work hard to get a good education, but is lost when she has her Ph.D.; or to have a dynamic career, and feels life is at an end when she retires. Most people tend to approximate to one of these scripts, both in overall life plan and in life style as reflected in their daily business. Stan Woollams gives some interesting examples of how sentence construction in conversations varies according to these scripts. There are some people who live one pattern of script at work and another at home — for example, an open-ended pattern at work and an 'until' pattern at home.

WHAT TO DO WITH YOUR SCRIPT

As the script is revealed, what can its owner do about it? Is it nothing more than an academic exercise? Is there any stage beyond the self-knowledge that comes with it? There are two important points to make here.

Firstly, a script has no magical qualities. It is not a mysterious entity buried deep in the individual's psyche. It is no more and no less than the messages that were given by ordinary everyday people to the young child and the decisions he made to cope with those messages. It is possible therefore to give yourself another set of messages to replace the original ones and make a new set of decisions about your life. The movement from one set of messages, given in childhood, to another given in maturity may not in practice be easy because the first set was given with potency and absorbed by a vulnerable child, subsequently to be re-inforced many times over the ensuing years. They have simply been around a long time. It might be necessary to utilise the help and strength that a TA group can give, or if you like expensive one-to-one relationships you could use a therapist. This can give the extra power and drive to compensate for the strength of the original messages.

Secondly, the decision of what to do with your life is yours alone. If you contemplate the script you have unravelled and decide it is not too bad to live with, that is your right. No one has the right to tell you that you ought to change.

However, before you decide to stay as you are, it is worth thinking about one of Eric Berne's fundamental insights. In a pointed phrase, he describes the baby as being born a prince or princess. It has no script. Its position is one of basic trust in the world. Before the child has been worked over by the people around him, he is a being capable of unqualified love, of spontaneous joy, and of straight thinking. It is the script which has twisted, perverted, limited, and destroyed those capacities in the grown adult, and it is the rediscovery of that potential which is the reward for those who begin to destroy their scripts.

FURTHER READING ON SCRIPTS

Nearly all books on TA say something about scripts, many say a great deal, but my own experience is that much of it confuses rather than helps. The following suggestions are based on what I have found particularly useful.

BERNE, Eric **What do you say after you say hello?** Corgi, 1975. ISBN 0-552-09806-X.

Not the book to start with, unless you find Berne's somewhat strange style easier to comprehend than I do, but it is important to know this is Berne's major book on scripts, and is where it all started. There is a script check list, pp. 427-439.

STEINER, C. **Games alcoholics play**. N.Y., Grave Press, 1971. ISBN 0-345-28470-4.

STEINER, C. **Scripts people live**. N.Y., Grave Press, 1974. ISBN 0-394-49267-6.

For me, these are the two key texts for understanding scripts. I think they are best read in this order. For those who wish to follow up the perception of scripts as loveless, joyless and mindless, the latter book is required reading.

JAMES, Muriel and Jangeward, Dorothy **Born to win**. Addison Wesley, 1977. ISBN 0-201-03311-9.

This very popular introduction to TA places great emphasis on scripts from the start of the book, and Chapter 4 presents their view of life scripts. I personally do not find their approach works well for me, but it does for other people and is certainly worth consulting. See also other of their books — **Winning with People**, pp. 1-15. **The People Book**, pp. 144-171.

WOOLLAMS, S. and Brown, M. **TA: the total handbook of transactional analysis**. Prentice-Hall, 1979. ISBN 0-13-881912-2.

I find this by far the most illuminating short account of scripts. The relevant chapters are 8 and 10.

Chapter 5

Assertive behaviour in relationships

In this chapter we look at some of the common situations that crop up week by week and are likely to cause particular difficulty or embarrassment in our relations with other people. Some of these we will handle with more comfort than others, but it is useful to be aware that even when we are skilful in handling a particular situation, it may be causing difficulties to many of our colleagues. The situations we will consider are the following:

1. **Dealing with bad service**
   For example, the shoddy goods we buy, the badly-prepared report we are given, the cold cup of coffee we are served, the poor quality repairs made to our car.

2. **Saying no**
   For example, dealing with door-to-door salesmen, with demands from colleagues, with sexual advances, with persistent profferers of food or drink.

3. **Facing prejudicial criticism or put-downs from others**
   Handling the attacks, barbs and nags from our work colleagues and from those we love as well as those who are our antagonists.

4. **Facing informed criticism from others**
   Handling critical comment which, whether we feel it is true or not, comes from the genuine belief of the other person and is presented in a relatively constructive (if somewhat clumsy) way.

5. **Confronting another person with your criticisms or negative feelings**
   Stating how we think or feel about another's actions or statements which are causing us concern or upset.

6. **Giving positive strokes to other people**
   Expressing our appreciation, admiration or thanks.

7. **Facing angry outbursts**
   Dealing with a tirade of abuse or a person shouting at us in anger.

There are skills and techniques which will improve the way we handle all these. Unfortunately a rational understanding of the techniques, and even some facility in practising them in a training workshop, will not be enough. It is not going to solve our problems. The trouble is that these kinds of situations hook into some very vulnerable parts of our personality. We fall very easily into feelings of guilt, anxiety and fear. Our past conditioning is all against us. We have been taught that we ought to be kind, helpful and considerate. We have been told many times not to make a fuss or be a nuisance. We have been criticised for being stupid or awkward or for causing embarrassment. We have been told not to be demanding or aggressive. Consequently many of us cannot easily assert ourselves and make a constructive and rational response based on the needs and possibilities of the situation. In TA terms, it is not our Adult that is activated, but out Adapted Child with its not-OK feelings.

When we respond to situations which activate such feelings, we are likely to fall into one of three kinds of behaviour.

> We can be **submissive**. We can agree to the demand, go along with the situation, justifying our stance to ourselves by saying that it doesn't really matter to us, or it isn't worth a fuss.

> We can be **passive but manipulative**, making people feel uncomfortable around us even though we actually accept the service or comply with the request.

> We can be **aggressive**. We can get worked up and angry, and engage in a fight. We determine to make sure no one takes us for a ride. We aim to win, but because we leave the incident with bad feelings (and very often later come-backs) our victory is very qualified.

The purpose of this chapter is to suggest that a fourth stance, that of being **assertive**, is the most satisfactory, least damaging, and most productive. Assertion training aims to increase our own self-esteem and self-respect, and hence our respect for others, by increasing our ability to respond assertively. Assertion is the capacity to express our ideas, opinions or feelings openly and directly without putting down ourselves or others. 'It involves standing up for your own rights in such a way that you do not violate another person's rights. It involves expressing thoughts, feelings and beliefs in direct, honest and appropriate ways.' It is neither an aggressive nor a defensive stance. It does not assume you can get what you want all of the time: indeed, it does not see interactions as being based on winning and losing. The assertive person is open to negotiations for workable compromises. It is a process of interacting which is not manipulative but straight.

It is easy to make such a series of statements about the value of assertion and believe in them. It is much more difficult to operate them consistently in practice, and no one is going to be able to do it all the time. We cannot always stop ourselves being manipulative nor prevent ourselves from being manipulated. For example, our rational conviction that it is a normal happening for anyone to make mistakes and we should therefore not feel guilty if it happens to us does not always hold up when our boss starts commenting on a particular error we have made. Nevertheless, assertion training can improve our capacity better to handle situations more often.

It is no good knowing the techniques of assertion unless we first accept our basic assertive rights as human beings. We need to accept them not as interesting hypotheses or part of a rationally defensible position, but as fundamental beliefs on which we build our lives. Assertive rights are formulated in slightly different ways by different people, and the following list incorporates statements from a number of sources.

LIST OF ASSERTIVE RIGHTS

1. **You are the ultimate judge of yourself**
   This is the prime human condition from which all else follows. It asserts that you are the ultimate judge of your own behaviour, thoughts and emotions, and take responsibility for their initiation and consequences on yourself. There will have been many people in everyone's life who have attempted to erode that right — parents, doctors, sons and daughters, clergymen, teachers, friends, politicians, enemies. There have been so many people telling any one individual what he is, what he should think, how well he is doing, what he should do. This right simply asserts that I make decisions about who I am, what I am worth, what I should do, how well I have done. It is not a selfish or irresponsible stance. It does not mean we do not listen to others, but it does mean that we do not give them power over us. If we are ultimately responsible for ourselves, we have no alibis, no way of blaming other people or outside events for our own lives.

2. **You have the right to make mistakes**
   Everyone does make mistakes, no one has the right to expect anyone to be perfect, so you have the right not to feel guilty when you make a mistake. You also have the right, of course, to face the consequences of your own mistakes.

3. **You have the right to say no**
   Not only have you the right to say no without feeling guilty, but you have the right not to have to justify yourself. You may decide you want to offer explanations but no one has the right to demand them of you. A demand for justification is generally a precursor to an attempted manipulation.

4. **You have the right to offer no reasons or excuses for your behaviour**
   It is **your** behaviour, not someone else's, and you have the freedom and right to decide on your behaviour without having to justify it. You may decide you wish to, or that in the circumstances it is reasonable to do so, but no one has the right to insist you do.

5. **You have the right to say 'I don't know'; to change your mind; to say 'I don't understand'**

6. **You have the right to say 'I don't care'**
   This is an important right, because it is by implying that you should care that guilt can be used as a manipulator by others. You are not required to care about everything or everyone, and if you choose not to care about your old aunt or endangered species of ducks, it is no one else's business. This is what Anne Dickson calls the compassion trap, and it is particularly relevant to women. You have the right to consider your own needs as well as those of others. 'Your needs are not necessarily more important than anyone else's needs — nor are they less important — just equally important.'

7. **You have the right not to take responsibility for solving other people's problems**
   However helpful you may wish to be, ultimately other people are in charge of their own problems, and you have a right to decide how far you wish to

53

become involved in them, if at all. Other people will probably try hard to drag you in, and manipulate your guilt feelings, but they have no right to off-load their problems on you.

8. **You have the right to express your feelings and opinions**
These are part of you, they do not need justifying or defending, and there is no reason why they should automatically be suppressed or discounted by you.

9. **You have a right to be treated with respect, listened to, and taken seriously**
If people are not prepared to do so, you have the right to assert this position. It is particularly important in boss-subordinate and male-female relationships where these rights are most likely to be denied.

It is very important that the meaning of asssertive rights is clearly understood. These are basic inalienable rights possessed simply by virtue of belonging to the human race. It does not mean that one should go round all the time looking for reasons to exercise them. There will be many times when people choose not to make a point of their rights. Situations are always specific and require sensitivity and common sense in response. The key work however is 'choice'. For the person secure in the understanding of her rights, the choice is real. She can choose to assert her rights, or to be passive and ride with it on any particular occasion.

Assertion training is about creating that freedom of movement, creating the capacity of choice, so that we are not the victims of the learned behaviour of our childhood and the manipulation of other people. With such choice we can operate in a way that is rewarding for us, but, as important, we can give proper respect to other people.

DEALING WITH BAD SERVICE
This section considers the techniques to be used in situations where we are faced with poor service when we are reasonably entitled to expect better. We may have taken receipt of a badly-cleaned coat, bought a steam-iron that does not work, been served with a pint of cloudy beer; at work we may have been given a shoddily-typed letter for our signature, or a report which has been hastily and badly compiled. We wish to return the coat to have it properly cleaned, to return the iron and have our money back, to have the letter properly retyped, and the report revised, and a reasonably clear glass glass of beer served to us. However, the other person involved will probably be concerned to avoid this outcome. He may do this in any of the following ways.

'It's not my responsibility'.
'I haven't the power to do anything'.
'It looks all right to me'.
'You must have done something to it yourself'.
'I'm over worked. It's the best I can do'.
'You're holding up other customers'.
'Come back later'.

All these are not legitimate responses. They attempt to avoid responsibility, induce guilt, offer alibis — in fact do anything but respond to the request. It is likely that we will be side-tracked by being hooked by one of these baits, and once we are hooked we are lost.

The technique to avoid this is known as 'broken record'. It consists simply of repeating your request over and over again, and avoiding any offered side-tracks. It is a very easy technique to use once it has been practised once or twice.

Lecturer: Deidre, I will need to have this letter retyped before I can sign it.

Deidre: I'm rushed off my feet today. Jean is away. So I can't find time getting everything dead right today.

Lecturer: I guess it is difficult, but I want the letter retyped.

Deidre: Couldn't you make the changes in pen. It would help me.

Lecturer: No, Deidre. I need the letter retyped.

Deidre: You know, Mr. Robinson, I wouldn't have had all this trouble if I'd had my new typewriter as I'd been promised.

Lecturer: Well, that must be very annoying for you, but I want the letter retyped.

Deidre: Oh well, I suppose you better leave it there. I'll try and get it done.

It is important to note the following characteristics of this exchange.

1. The lecturer did not respond to and take up any of the excuses, complaints or other traps, other than simply by indicating he had heard what the typist had said.
2. He did nothing else but repeat, with assertion and without aggression, his request for the letter to be retyped.
3. In order to be able to do that, he needed to believe he had a right to have the letter properly typed. If he was at all wavering about that in his mind, he would find it difficult to persist so single-mindedly with his request.
4. The lecturer remained calm and uncritical. It is essential in this technique of broken record that no critical parent statements are introduced. For example if the lecturer had said at some stage:

   'Look, it's your job to type letters properly. I shouldn't have to come and tell you.'

   then the typist no longer needs to think of diversionary statements herself. He has done the job for her, and she can happily get away from the main issue of retyping the letter by following up the criticism, e.g.:

   'What right have you got to tell me my job?'

If the lecturer keeps to the technique of broken record as outlined above, then in the end (and it may require some persistence)' the typist is faced very baldly with a situation where she has to decide either to retype the letter or refuse to do so. All other diversionary avenues have been avoided.

You might ask what happens if both parties are assertive and practice the technique of broken record. Who wins? The purpose of assertion is not to win but to reach a situation which satisfies your right to expect reasonable service, and the solution can be a negotiated workable compromise. This would be absolutely necessary if both parties were assertive, and is likely to be the solution even when that is not the case. Being assertive does not mean driving through life as a winner, leaving behind scores of defeated adversaries. A workable compromise to the interchange given above might be as follows.

| Typist: | OK, I will type it again. It is a bit shoddy. But I must get this report done for the registrar to catch the post. If your letter is not urgent can I do it after that and risk missing the post? |
| Lecturer: | That's fine. A day won't make any difference. |

There are several examples of interchanges using broken record techniques in the books by Manuel Smith and Anne Dickson referenced at the end of this chapter. You can practice the technique by role-playing some of the situations referred to at the start of this section with a colleague.

SAYING NO

A colleague asks if he can borrow a book — you don't want to let it out of your possession.

A neighbour asks you to babysit — you don't want to do it.

A fellow student asks to borrow your assignment to copy — you don't approve of that.

A close friend asks you to go to bed with him — you like him but don't want a sexual relationship.

Your parents ask you to stay with them at Christmas — you want to go somewhere else.

A salesman wants you to buy a set of encyclopaedias — you don't want them.

An acquaintance wants to buy you a 'real' drink — you want an orange juice.

Saying no to requests is something we all find difficult sometimes. Each individual will find it easy with some people over some issues, but often enough with other people and other issues it is hard, and if it is done it probably leaves us feeling guilty.

To whom is it most difficult for you to say no — the salesman at the door, the stranger, a work colleague, your boss, a lover or spouse, your parents, your children? It will vary for different people, but in general it becomes more difficult the closer we are to a person. It is when we want to say no that manipulation of learned childhood feelings is most pervasive. Many of us carry around a collection of feelings and beliefs which resembles the following.

Saying no will hurt or upset people.
Saying no is self-centred and uncaring.
Saying no will make people not like me.
Saying no on small things looks petty and inflexible.
Saying no directly will make me look rude and abrupt.

Behind these statements is a belief that other people are more important than I — I am not entitled to put my own wishes first. If I do, it is quite proper I should feel bad about it. This is such a pervasive problem that it is not surprising two of the best-selling books on assertion training are called: **Don't Say Yes When You Want To Say No,** and **When I Say No, I Feel Guilty**.

In order to recover the freedom to say no when you want to, it is critical to internalise two beliefs.

'I have a right to say No'.
'When I say no, I refuse the request, not reject the person'.

Many people find it very difficult to accept these. They go against years of conditioning and training.

The basic technique for saying no to persistent requests, is the use of 'broken record'. It will be more difficult than in insisting on good service because the potentialies for manipulation are greater.

Bill:	Hi, Barbara, are you going to the staff dance?
Barbara:	No.
Bill:	How about coming with me? I've got no one to go with.
Barbara:	No, thanks.
Bill:	Oh, come on. You work too hard, and don't go out nearly enough.
Barbara:	No, I really don't want to go.
Bill:	It will do you good, you know — a bit of fun and relaxation.
Barbara:	I haven't really got the time.
Bill:	You know, people will be seeing you as a dull, frowsy thing if you never join in anything. Why don't you make time for this?
Barbara:	I just don't feel like it.
Bill:	Quite a few people can't go. It could be a bit of a flop if we all opt out. I don't really fancy it, but I think we ought to go and support it.
Barbara:	Well, we don't have to go. It's not compulsory.
Bill:	Look, Barbara. I'll be honest with you. Since my wife died last year, I have hardly been out at all. I've not wanted to. But I really want to make the effort this time, and I thought you, as an old friend, might help.
Barbara:	Well, if you put it like that. . . .

If Bill couldn't get her one way, he would get her another. As she gradually weakens and loses touch with the broken record, his chance of getting her to accept, or alternatively of getting her to lose her temper, becomes very high.

Apart from holding on to the broken record technique, there are one or two practices that will very often help in saying no.

Ask for more information about what is involved before giving an answer. This is not always appropriate, but if someone has asked you to give a lecture you can ask for details about what is expected, when it will start and finish, what is the fee, etc., before saying yes or no.

Ask for time to think about it. No one has the right to expect an immediate answer of you, and to ask even in a formal meeting for a few minutes to think about a request is a totally reasonable response.

Don't give excuses for your refusal. A polite but firm no is all that is needed, and excuses will only cloud and confuse the interchange and reduce you from being assertive to being apologetic. Very often it is clear to both parties that the excuses are not genuine. Remember that one of your basic rights is of saying no without having to justify it.

Do not hang around. There is a strange phenomenon that after we have turned down a request, we feel some necessity to stay around the person. It probably arises from our need for assurance that our refusal will not be followed by personal rejection, or our worry that we have hurt the other person in some way. It is part of our guilt about saying no. The general rule is that after refusing a request, we move away unless there is other business to transact, unless it is socially clearly inappropriate, or unless our common sense tells us that it is important to stay.

Take personal responsibility for saying no. It keeps the transaction cleaner and less liable to manipulation if you say 'I don't want to' or 'I don't feel like it', rather than 'I can't' or 'my parents wouldn't approve'.

Practice saying 'no'. For some people, the word 'no' is a remarkably difficult one to use, and they will engage in all sorts of verbal contortions to avoid saying it, even when refusing a request. It is valuable to practice saying the word, hearing what it sounds like, and getting used to what it feels like, until a greater level of comfort and familiarity is reached.

We conclude this section by repeating a sentence which exposes the heart of the problem:

'You refuse the request, not reject the person'.

If that can be fully accepted, saying no ceases to be a problem of great import.

FACING PREJUDICIAL COMMENTS OR PUT-DOWNS FROM OTHERS

We all face at times the stings and arrows from the armoury of our associates. Sometimes these can form a substantial part of a relationship between two people such as a husband and wife or two neighbours. The comments are designed to hurt and put-down the other person, and can vary in intensity from a slight barb to the thrust that cuts to the quick. It is easy after the event to say that the attack was childish and inaccurate and we should not take any notice of it. At the time, however, it is remarkably difficult to avoid being hooked into not-OK Child feelings and responding aggressively or defensively. We may strike back at the person, we may try to justify or excuse ourselves, we may sulk or even burst into tears. It is not in the reflective and considered analysis of what happened subsequent to the event that assertion techniques can help. It is concerned with techniques needed at the moment prejudicial comments are made. We are at that moment very vulnerable. We are experiencing rejection, for ipso facto prejudicial statements to us are that. We are probably being labelled — as useless, selfish, just like your father. We may well be worrying that we are being over-sensitive to the comments of others. In the face of this vulnerability, it is well to recall the first and prime of our assertive rights.

You have the right to be the ultimate judge of yourself. It is worth trying to hold on to the belief that other people's approval, while pleasant, is not essential to our happiness and well-being. Such basic values, however, tend to be elusive when they are most needed, and assertion techniques help us to cope while they are recovered.

The key technique is **Fogging**. The basis of fogging is to avoid the three commonplace responses:

1. Do not deny any criticism.
2. Do not defend yourself.
3. Do not counter-attack with criticism of the other person.

Fogging is a way of de-activating criticism by giving it no surface against which to strike. You cannot hit a fog bank with a stone. There are four ways of doing this.

1. The criticised person can agree with any truth in the statements made against her, e.g.:

> Fred: 'You were late in the office yet again this morning, Jane. You are so unreliable.'
>
> Jane: 'That's true. I was late in the office this morning.'

2. The criticised person can agree with any possible truth in the statements, as possibilities.

> Fred: 'You'll be in trouble with the manager.'
>
> Jane: 'You could be right. I might be in trouble.'

3. The criticised person can agree with any general truths in any logical statements made to her.

> Fred: 'If you get in at this time, you'll get behind with your work and might miss your upgrading. Or we'll find ourselves having to help you out.'
>
> Jane: 'You're right. That makes sense. So if I think I'm getting behind hand, I'll make the time to catch up.'

4. The criticised person can acknowledge the perceptions of the critic without accepting their factual truth. After all, he has a right to his perceptions.

> Fred: 'You're irresponsible. You don't seem to care about anything.'
>
> Jane: 'I expect I must seem that way to you sometimes.'

The value of fogging is that in the end, and sooner rather than later, the critic will give up because he is getting back no solid material on which to continue his attack. There is no denial, no attempted justification, no counter-attack — nothing but insubstantial fog. Although on the first few occasions the person using this technique may feel some dissatisfaction in that there seems to be no constructive outcome, the effect is cumulative. When anyone's attempted manipulation of another person fails to produce the expected effect, and is met by an assertive rather than an aggressive or defensive approach, then interactions and exchanges begin to get cleaned up. Being fogged constantly is not a pleasant experience, and people involved in habitual relationships may well begin to reduce the put-down comments which might lead to fogging.

Fogging can be reinforced by another technique, **Negative Enquiry**. This is particularly relevant to relationships of some duration and closeness. Negative Enquiry involves breaking the cycle of manipulation by asking for more criticism or more information about the behaviour at issue. Note that this is not what the criticiser expects — he is waiting for a denial, a defence or a counter-attack.

> John: 'You've been sitting around reading that book all day.'
>
> Mary: (Alternative A — denial.) 'That's not true. I did the shopping this morning and I cleaned up the guest room.'
>
> Mary: (Alternative B — defence.) 'Well, I want to get it back to the library because there will be a fine on it if I don't, so I'm going to catch up with my work this evening, or get up early tomorrow, and . . .
>
> Mary: (Alternative C — attack.) 'So what. You've been fiddling with that stupid motorbike all day — that's when you haven't been asleep in front of the telly.'

Mary: (Negative Enquiry.) 'What is it about me reading this book that is making you unhappy?'

John: 'You must have better things to do.'

Mary: (Negative Enquiry.) 'I don't understand. What better things do you think I should be doing?'

John: 'Well, you could spend more time on housework.'

Mary: (Negative Enquiry.) 'What is the work I haven't done that is upsetting you?'

John: 'Well, for instance, why don't you cook more instead of reading so much?'

Mary: (Negative Enquiry.) 'I don't understand. What do you think I should be cooking instead of reading?'

John: 'Well, you could have cooked a proper lunch today instead of throwing together a cold salad. You know I hate salad.'

The key points about this dialogue are:

1. Mary behaved as if the criticism was not something to get upset about.
2. Mary used negative enquiry throughout. Had she defended, denied or attacked, the conversation would have followed a different course.
3. This established whether there was any substance in the initial criticism or whether it masked another issue. She obtained further information in amplification of the criticism.
4. In this case, it was not the fact that Mary was reading, but the absence of a hot meal which had upset John. Once that was established, there was a chance that a workable compromise could be found.

There is a fundamental issue exemplified here. There is no reason why John should not feel angry about being given a cold salad which he hates rather than a hot meal. This is an honest feeling which he does not need to justify to anyone, but if he wants some changes to take place that involve other people, then he has got to state how he feels and discuss the possibilities of a workable compromise. To do this, however, he has to come out with what is really annoying him and not attack Mary for some quite unconnected behaviour. It is not legitimate for him to use his hurt feelings to attack Mary's right to read a book or to spend her time in any other way she wants. Such a manipulation is imposing on other people an arbitrary right-and-wrong structure that tells them what they can or cannot do. Negative Enquiry breaks into this and helps people state their real concerns and bothers, thus enabling constructive actions to follow.

FACING INFORMED CRITICISM FROM OTHERS

Included in this section is well-intended criticism even if it is not particularly informed. The situation differs from that in the preceeding section in that the criticism is made from genuine belief in its accuracy and presented in a relatively supportive and constructive way. That is the intention even if in the event comments are clumsily expressed or sound somewhat abrupt. The key technique in dealing with such criticism is to accept that part which is or may be true without feeling guilt or the need to explain and justify.

Camilla: 'Well, Sally, I'm sorry to say but you really made a mess of that presentation.'

Sally: 'You're right. I fouled it up.'

It is certainly not easy to accept and agree with criticism without feeling the accompanying guilt. It is important to hold on to the basic right that you have to make mistakes without feeling guilty. It does not mean, however, that criticism should be treated lightly. You are also responsible for your actions.

Henry: 'Sorry, David, but you really made a mess of that presentation. I don't know what will happen now.'

David: 'You're right. I fouled it up. I will have to think how to retrieve the situation.'

Sometimes the criticiser cannot leave the matter alone and is thrown by the lack of guilt feelings in the response. If your assertive acceptance of your error or shortcoming is not heard and honoured after several statements, it may be necessary to reinforce it with fogging or negative enquiry. The basic message of this section, however, is that criticism is accepted for what it is — an accurate statement about a shortcoming or mistake — and that is all it is accepted for. There is no acceptance of guilt or of any washover effects from the actual point criticised to the rest of your personality and actions.

If the criticism is in your opinion not accurate, then you have the choice of two strategies.

1. You can accept it as a statement of the other person's opinion.

Eric: 'Do you really think you should wear jeans for a meeting like this?'

Ron: 'Thanks for giving me your opinion.' (An American would probably add — 'I appreciate that.')

2. You can assertively deny the criticisms.

Judy: 'You haven't been very constructive in our committee meetings.'

Rachel: 'I don't agree. I believe I have been helpful.'

This needs to be said with conviction, without apology or attack, and with the appropriate body language. The self-deprecating smile or flush of anger will destroy the spoken message.

Both strategies can be followed: a statement of recognition of the other person's opinion, followed by an assertive denial of the criticism. To summarise, when facing constructive criticism the recipient:

1. Recognises the right of the other person to give criticism;
2. Responds assertively, i.e., neither defensively nor aggressively and certainly not emotionally;
3. Accepts criticism which he sees as valid;
4. Does not accept criticism which he sees as invalid, but acknowledges it as the opinion of the other person.
5. When he feels it is needed, asserts a contrary statement.

CONFRONTING OTHERS WITH CRITICISM AND FEEDBACK

Consider the following situations:
1. You have found the behaviour and contributions of a colleague very unconstructive in a working party you chair. You want her to behave more constructively.

2. You are the recipient of sexist remarks from a male colleague and wish the other person to know of your annoyance and stop his behaviour.
3. You find the way your secretary greets your visitors very unhelpful to the subsequent interview and want her to alter her approach.
4. You are angry the way blacks were referred to in a staffroom conversation and wish to express your disapproval.

In these and similar situations, which are likely to occur day by day, we are faced with the need to confront other people critically with their behaviour. Whether in social, family or work-settings, how can we feed back to people our messages without giving unnecessary hurt to them, embarrassment to ourselves, or compromise of the essential substance of the criticism? It is a minefield and many people avoid the danger by not confronting others unless they are absolutely forced to. We have to accept that there is not any way we can give critical feedback and expect the recipient or ourselves to feel very happy about it. What we are aiming at is an exchange in which we feel relatively comfortable and the recipient is able to hear the message without experiencing aggressive attack or being hooked into Child feelings of anger or fear. The exchange is not to satisfy our own feelings of self-righteousness or to get things out of our system. It is to help ourselves and the other person to clean up a relationship which is contaminated in some way.

We need to start with some guidelines.

1. Provided that we present our criticism as fairly, skilfully and sensitively as we can, we are not in the end responsible for the behaviour of the recipient. It is his choice how he reacts to the criticism, and if he is angry or upset about it the giver should not feel guilty about it.
2. Making judgements about other people is counter-productive. Statements such as 'you never think things out properly' or 'you always rush into things without preparation' are of no help to the recipient and are only likely to annoy him.
3. Labelling people by name or trait is not legitimate. It would be difficult to justify by analysis any label given. Furthermore labelling is counter-productive in that it is likely to activate strong feelings in the other person which will lead to rejection of the message being given. Statements such as 'you are authoritarian', 'you are old-fashioned', 'you are a layabout' need to be avoided.
4. It is unhelpful to attribute motives to other people. There is no way in which we can know the motives of others. They are certainly likely to be much more complex than can be encompassed in a single accusation. Statements such as, 'You can't be bothered', 'You're only interested in the money', or 'All you are after is status' are unjustifiable by any criteria.
5. The focus should be on the value of the feedback to the receiver, not the release of the feelings of the provider. It would be unrealistic to pretend that there was not sometimes some release of frustration, but that is not where the focus should lie.
6. The aim of feedback should be to give to the receiver specific information that is publicly available for consideration, i.e., it is not inferred, it is not

judgemental, but it is behaviour that was observable. Thus feedback should concentrate on:

What the recipient did;
What he said (not why he said it);
Objective observations (without making inferences);
What the provider thinks happened;
Giving any other relevant information.

7. As a general rule, statements should be 'more or less' rather than black and white, tentative rather than certain. 'You don't seem very worried,' is a very different statement from 'You never care about anything or anyone.'

8. As part of the giving of specific information, the provider can reveal his own feelings. 'I am angry about . . . I am frustrated by . . .' Disclosure of feelings is an essential part of confrontation techniques, but this must be done so that it is not manipulative of the other person. Its purpose is not to make him feel guilty or stupid. It is a statement about you, not about him, and it is presented simply as a fact in the situation. If feelings are not freely disclosed, they will appear covertly in the exchange and contaminate it in some way or other. If, for example, you are very angry about another person's behaviour and suppress this when talking to him about it, it is very unlikely the course of the exchange will be honest and straightforward, nor the outcome constructive.

9. Feedback should be not presented so apologetically or so wrapped up in conditional and qualifying statements that the message is lost. Assertive feedback is not aggressive, but it is to the point.

10. Feedback should lead to a negotiated outcome whenever possible and should therefore contain a statement of desired change. As part of the exchange it should normally invite comment, which the recipient may or may not choose to give, on his reactions to the feedback.

THE FIVE-STAGE MESSAGE

If these guidelines are accepted, a strategy for critical feedback can be developed from them. The strategy involves five separate parts to the message.

Stage 1. **Objective identification of the other person's behaviour:**
e.g. 'Your handing in of this report later than 10 am . . .'
Stage 2. **The tangible effect of the behaviour on me:**
e.g. 'Causes me to have to rush to get my report in by noon. Sometimes my report is late.'
Stage 3. **My feelings about that:**
e.g. 'And I feel quite frustrated and bothered about that.'
Stage 4. **My request for behaviour changes:**
e.g. 'I would like you to get your report in on time.'
Stage 5. **Invitation to other person to comment:**
e.g. 'How do you react to that?'

This is a model, and like all models will not suit all situations without adaptation. For some confrontation situations it may not be relevant to indicate a behaviour change or to invite comment but in most cases it will be, and on occasions there may not be tangible effects that are distinct from one's feelings. If these stages are followed, however, with whatever adaptations seem appropriate, then there is likely to be a successful outcome. In the example given above there is no judgement, labelling or attribution of motives. There is a focus on specific behaviour, on the provider's feelings, and on clearly stated requests.

If we refer back to the situations outlined at the beginning of this section, we can consider some typical responses using the five part message. We may wish to use an initial phrase to gain the listener's attention.

Example 1

'The way you attacked everyone's suggestions at the meeting today caused us to make no progress to a solution. That frustrates me as I have wasted valuable time. I would like you to spend more time presenting your own ideas and less time criticising other people's. How do you feel about what I have said?'

Example 2

'Please listen very carefully. Your reference to my sex seems to me to treat me like a child or plaything. That makes me feel very angry and abused. I would like you to stop making references to my sex. What are your reactions to what I have just said?'

Example 3

'There is something of importance to me I want to say to you. The way you referred to blacks upset me so much that I walked out of the staffroom. I would like you not to do it. How do you react to my feelings?'

Example 4

'Because you do not smile at visitors to the office and greet them in a friendly way I am having some problems putting them at ease. This makes me impatient and annoyed. I would like you to put some effort into welcoming visitors over the next few days and than have a review with you. How do you feel about what I have said?'

The confrontation must of course be done with perception and sensitivity to the person and the occasion. It is important to choose carefully the time and place for confrontation. Sometimes it has to be given immediately; on other occasions it is worth waiting a short time. Sometimes it is not appropriate to invite comment back, as for example might be true of situations similar to the second and third examples given above. There will be occasions when it is worth staying around to explore responses, there are others when it is most appropriate to walk away immediately. Each situation has to be judged separately. Nevertheless, the general strategy does not alter. Confrontation feedback involves

His behaviour,
your problem and needs,
your request;
not his character or personality,
his problem and needs,
your invitation to a combat.

DEALING WITH THE ANGRY OUTBURST

What can you do when faced with someone who is worked up into an angry state and engaged in a tirade of accusation or abuse? It is a situation many people find frightening or embarrassing and is never the easiest to deal with. There are two basic points to remember from the start.

1. You should not accept that you are the cause of the anger and therefore feel guilty or defensive. He is responsible for his angry behaviour and it may have many causes which are nothing to do with you. He may for example have in TA terms an anger racket and is simply using situations as they arise to satisfy his needs, or he may be displacing anger from another relationship or problem altogether. Whatever the causes, they are mostly likely to lie within the person himself.
2. Every person has the right to walk away from anyone who is shouting or storming at them. That is a basic right and it can be exercised assertively at any stage of the encounter. Everyone has the right to shout at someone else, but they have not the right to expect them to stay put.

It may be, however, that you want to try and work through the situation with him. Walking away from the problem would be less constructive than facing it. If that is the case, then the purpose of any action must be to engage in a two-way exchange rather than be at the receiving end of an emotional outburst. It is necessary to calm the person down sufficiently to enable an interaction to start. It is important to accept that the purpose of calming a person is not to reduce levels of embarrassment or tension, nor to suppress what needs to be said. The technique of achieving this shift from monologue to interaction is not an easy one and calls for all one's assertive beliefs. Anne Dickson suggests that the following sequence of actions will often work.

1. The first step is to gain the person's attention by repeating a phrase over and over again, loud enough to be heard but without shouting. You might use his name or a phrase such as 'please listen to me', or 'I have something to say to you.'
2. The second step is to catch his eye. This will generally happen if you have been persistent enough with the repetitive phrase. As soon as you make eye contact, try to hold it.
3. There will be a slight pause as he registers eye contact. It may be very brief indeed so you will need to be ready with a phrase that you can produce instantly. The phrase needs to consist of three parts:

    a recognition of the other person's anger;
    an expression of your own reactions to his anger;
    a statement of willingness to co-operate in looking for a solution.

    An appropriate sentence might be:

    'I can see you are very angry and that makes me feel rather apprehensive, but I would like to hear what you have to say so that we can work out a solution.'

You may have to go through these first three steps more than once before they make an impact and an interchange starts. Persistence, patience and resistance to feelings of anger, guilt or fear are the required behaviours and they are not easy in the face of a red-faced man beside himself with anger and shouting at the top of his voice. However, once an interchange starts, the tirade of anger will quickly lose its force. The very process of listening, however grudgingly or briefly, will change the tone and probably the volume of his output.

4. The fourth step is to endeavour to get him to sit down if he is standing up, and lower his voice. This is done by talking quietly and calmly yourself and issuing an invitation such as, 'Why don't we sit down and see if we can talk about what happened?' He may not sit down, but it is worth a try.
5. The fifth step is to use active listening skills to hear out what he has to say, reflecting back his statements, giving non-verbal attention and as many supportive cues as possible. At this stage it is important to move nearer to him. At the beginning of the encounter, you are likely to be at a fairly wide distance apart as is normal for this kind of situation. By this stage, the distance between the two of you and the posture you adopt should be that normal for counselling interviews. This in itself will have a marked effect.
6. The final step will follow when he feels that you have properly recognised his immediate concerns and feelings, and have listened carefully and supportively to him. It is then possible to move, if it is appropriate, to joint problem-solving.

It is important to be ready at any time during the encounter to admit your own contribution to the problem, however slight it might be.

'Perhaps I was not very sympathetic dealing with that matter the other day. I was too absorbed with my own concerns.'

It is a matter of considered timing to decide when you make such statements. There is little point until he is at least likely to hear and record what you say. Attention to non-verbal presentation is vital throughout the interview. If we feel angry or overwhelmed or persecuted then we might control carefully our verbal responses along the lines suggested above, but facial gestures, our bodily posture, the tone of our voice may give away our true feelings. The clenched fist or the apologetic smile destroys the assertive stance. Control of voice is a particularly powerful aid in encounters of this type. The quiet, firm voice consistently used throughout will do much on its own to change the other person's behaviour.

It would be unduly optimistic to pretend that following the approach outlined here will always lead to a satisfactory outcome. Some encounters will be unmanageable: some will end in confusion or with angry feelings unabated. But following the above approach will make such outcomes less likely. It is an assertive response in that it openly accepts the other person's anger, declares the recipient's feelings and seeks for a solution by co-operation and concern. It is not a response based on aggression, defensiveness or submission.

RECEIVING AND GIVING APPRECIATION MESSAGES

Chapter 2 discussed the giving and receiving of strokes. It was there suggested that increasing the number and variety of strokes given and learning to accept without discounting the strokes received would make considerable difference to any person's interpersonal experiences. The following comments are a coda to that section.

There is some skill in expressing appreciation to someone. However it is done it will do some good, but its impact can be much increased if it is done well. The least effective stroke is the very general or very globalised message. 'You're doing a grand job', or 'You've all done very well' are pleasant statements to receive but are too abstract and remote to be very highly valued. The stroke that is most appreciated is one:

> that is addressed to one specific person;
> that indicates the specific behaviour or situation which you appreciate;
> which indicates the tangible effect it has had on you;
> which expresses your feelings about the other person.

For example:

> 'I'm very grateful to you for taking my lecture yesterday. It enabled me to complete a difficult interview successfully and I am really happy about that.'

> 'Your dealing with the visit of the training officer while I was away was a great success. He was very pleased with the outcome, and I really appreciate what you did.'

Such messages are clearly much more valued than:

> 'Thank you for all you've done.'

It is repetitive, but nevertheless important to emphasise once again that body language should be totally congruent with the verbal message. To express appreciation of a specific action while gathering up your papers, looking at the clock, or gazing out of the window takes away half of the effect.

The skill of receiving appreciation messages is not to discount them but to accept them. You may however decide not to accept a message as it stands because you suspect it is manipulative or crooked or is given without any real thought. You may indeed find the message offensive and assertively reject it. For example:

> 'You have a gorgeous body.'
> 'That remark makes me feel very angry. I want to ask you not to make remarks about my physical appearance.'

If you feel that an appreciation message is given with good will but without sufficient thought, you can pursue it assertively which will have the effect of giving you a clearer idea of what it is the other person appreciates and at the same time help him learn to give strokes more skilfully. For example:

> 'You're doing a grand job.'
> 'Thank you. What is it in particular you think I am doing well? It would help me if I knew that.'

Such a response exposes the plastic stroke or manipulative message of appreciation and expands the real but half-expressed appreciation message.

SUMMARY
The assertive person has the freedom to choose a behaviour which is neither aggressive nor submissive.

The assertive person is aware of his rights as a human being and is judiciously selective in affirming those rights. The confidence in his own worth that his assertion of his rights gives him enables him to develop techniques for effectively handling a variety of confronting situations — giving and receiving criticism, obtaining proper service, dealing with anger, refusing requests.

The assertive person, because he relates openly and honestly and does not discount his own needs, respects and honours the rights and independence of others. Assertion is therefore a stance which helps the process of creative development, of free and autonomous relationships, and of productive work.

FURTHER READING

SMITH, M., **When I say no I feel guilty**. Dial, 1975. ISBN 0-553-13715-8.

FENSTERNHEIM, H. and BAER, J., **Don't say yes when you want to say no**. Futura, 1976. ISBN 0-8600-7437-4.

These two American best-sellers present most of the thinking and techniques related to assertiveness training. They both contain many sample dialogues in various problem situations. The first is particularly thorough in its discussion of assertive rights. They are written with American culture and life-style in mind and I find rather more aggression and concern with winning (in spite of disclaimers in the books) than I would like.

There is a training film based on the first book, marketed by Training Films International, of Whitchurch, Shropshire, also entitled:

When I say no I feel guilty.

DICKSON, Anne, **A woman in your own right**. Quartet, 1982. ISBN 0-7043-3420-8.

This is an excellent book and the best introduction now on the market. It is written by an English psychologist and counsellor who has done much to develop assertiveness training in this country. Although it specifically explores assertiveness from the woman's position and is a powerful critique of a sexist society, everything it says about human relationships and techniques for assertive living in equally applicable to men.

BACK, Ken and Kate. **Assertiveness at work — a practical guide to handling awkward situations**. McGraw-Hill, 1982. ISBN 0-07-084576-X.

This is another very good recent introduction.

Chapter 6

Non-verbal behaviour

INTRODUCTION

One of the ways we communicate with other people is by speech. We often think of this as the major, if not the only, way in which we can make ourselves understood. We concentrate on putting our words together in such a way that our meaning is absolutely clear. We hope our speech conveys exactly the meaning we want it to convey.

Yet this is only a part, and the less important part, of the communication process, Non-verbal mechanisms of communication have a much greater impact on us than verbal ones. Animals, indeed, have to communicate entirely non-verbally, and have an extensive repertoire of signs for doing this.

Normally verbal and non-verbal messages support each other in an interactive way. We say:

'I like being with you.'

We support this with an open smile and movement nearer to our respondent. She hears the words, but it is the non-verbal signs that really get the message over. She is convinced by the smile, not the meaning of the five words. If the word meaning is contradicted by non-verbal signs, however, it is the latter we believe. If we say:

'I like being with you.'

but our smile never reaches our eyes, which remain cold or hostile, and we lean backwards with our body stiff and tense, then our respondent will not believe we like being with them. Words have an unequal fight with non-verbal signs. When we try to recall social exchanges, such as an interview for a job, we find it much more difficult to remember the words spoken than our perceptions about how people were acting towards us — in a friendly or hostile or concerned way, for example.

One of the major differences between verbal and non-verbal communication is that verbal messages are conscious and pre-thought while non-verbal messages very frequently are not. Both the giver and receiver are often not conscious of what is passing between them. A frequently quoted example of this is eye pupil dilation. When one person feels attracted to another his eye pupil will dilate, and this in turn is a very powerful signal of attraction to the receiver. Neither, however, will be aware of the giving or receiving of a message that is establishing a bond between them.

THE MECHANISMS OF NON-VERBAL COMMUNICATION

We can divide these mechanisms into those associated with the tactile, visual, auditory and olefactory senses.

Tactile Communication

Sending messages by means of touch is limited by strong taboos or conventions about body contact found in most societies or cultures. The English are not prone to much body contact except in certain stylised forms (e.g. handshakes) or special relationships (e.g. between lovers). Most European peoples touch more than the English, though the English touch more than, for example, the Indians. We can divide tactile messages into:—

(i)   those concerned with hitting or other agressive contact
(ii) those concerned with caressing or stroking
(iii) those concerned with greeting people or saying farewell
(iv) those concerned with guiding another person's movements

Visual Communication

We can divide these messages into seven types.

Proximity. The nearness or distance which people take towards each other indicates the way they are feeling towards them. Generally the more a person likes another, or the more interested he is in what he is saying or doing, the closer he moves to him. Conversely people who do not want to convey intimacy, interest or friendship keep their distance.

Orientation. The way in which a person handles the space around him and positions himself in relation to others gives various messages. Asking someone to sit next to you gives a different relationship to sitting opposite them with a desk in between. A teacher can sit behind a desk on a dais in front of the class, or he can sit in a circle of chairs with his students. A housewife can stand at the door and talk to a salesman or she can ask him in to sit down. All variations of positioning and placing are making statements to the recipient.

Posture. The way a person stands or sits, and particularly the way he holds his back and shoulders, gives very clear messages reflecting anger, dominance, impatience, defeat or depression, alertness, etc. Very often it is possible to tell what mood a person is in before we see his features or hear his voice by the way he stands. Careful observation of changes of posture of a member in committee give clear messages of what he thinks about what is being said or who is saying it.

Physical Appearance. We make decisions about how we appear to other people. We control our clothes, our hair, to some extent through the use of cosmetics our skin and nails. We generally make these decisions on the basis of what image we want to portray and how we want other people to perceive us. The clothes we wear for any specific occasion give clues about how we see the occasion and how we intend to relate to the people there. Most obviously, this operates along the dimension of formality-informality. To some extent we can manipulate our appearance during a meeting by taking off our jacket or shoes, ruffling our hair, or loosening our tie.

Gaze
Facial Expressions } These particularly important mechanisms will be given more extended treatment below.
Gestures

Auditory Communication

Apart from the actual meaning of words, we convey many messages in our speech by the tone of voice we use (which may belie the words themselves), our

70

accent, timing and stress of speech rhythms, and speed of delivery. Of these by far the most powerful in impact is the tone of voice which can communicate emotional states, but generally all the various factors work together. For example, if someone is conveying excitement in his tone of voice, this will also affect the speed of his speech.

Olefactory Communication

Animals use smell extensively in their communications, giving off different smells for special purposes. It is likely that humans do the same — we do after all talk about the smell of fear — but our sense of smell has become much weakened in the course of evolution, and it may now play a relatively unimportant part in communications except when deliberately manipulated by the use of artificial smells. The use of scents and perfumes of one sort or another is a very conscious way of passing messages about oneself.

THREE KEY MECHANISMS

Gaze. This is a very powerful means of communication. It is odd that it is both a channel of communication — i.e. a way of seeing things, and a transmitter of messages since the very act of looking at something implies an act of recognition of some sort.

Long gazes (that is of more than six seconds) generally indicate very high degrees of intimacy and liking, and are normally associated with other signs such as touching or close proximity. The more a person is deprived of these other signs in such a situation, the longer tends to be his gaze. Long gazes can also be used to indicate other strong feelings such as aggression.

Shorter glances of under six seconds are used for various purposes. Commonly they are used at the end of an utterance, in order to check on how it has been received. This terminal glance is also used as a synchronisation device to indicate the intention of pausing, so the next speaker knows when to come in.

Glances can be used as specific signals. They are frequently used to indicate to another person across the room a willingness to enter into an interaction, and the recipient responds with a glance signifying agreement, or looks away signifying unwillingness. Glances can also be used to catch a chairman's eye, or to make a bid at an auction.

During a conversation between two people, the exchange of looks on average occupies between 25% and 75% of each of their time. During some of this time, they will both be looking at each other, something like 15% to 50% of their time. People look more when they are listening than when they are talking (generally about twice as much), and look away most often when unsure of what they are saying or finding its expression difficult.

Gestures. There is a vocabulary of gesture which is fairly well understood throughout all cultures. A beckoning gesture can, for example, be recognised almost anywhere in the world, as can pointing for the purposes of directing someone's attention to an object. Each society also develops very specific gestures which have meaning only to that particular society. The number of these vary very much from one society to another. In this country we have about 20 but in Naples there are something like 200. There are also some specialised gesture languages used where speech is not possible, for example in broadcasting studios or on race tracks.

One of the major functions of gesture therefore seems to be to supplement the meaning of our words by emphasis or clarification, or replacing speech where it is not possible.

Involuntary gestures in apparently pointless body movements, such as clenching fists or tapping feet indicate emotional arousal. Frequently such gestures indicate anxiety or worry, but they can also indicate aggression, tiredness or concern for someone. Such gestural clues are important in estimating whether the meaning of the words is congruent with the feelings of the speaker. The man who is accepting blame for a failure with apparent good grace may show by the clenching of his fists and other signs that he is really very angry indeed.

Facial Expressions. The face can display many different kinds of feelings. It can indicate anger, suffering, happiness, contempt, fear, etc. When people make no attempt to control their facial muscles, then we normally see very clearly these feelings, but very often we do exercise some control. We wish in most company to guard ourselves from too much revelation of our feelings, and so we may smile sweetly while seething with fury inside. It is also the case that there are some differences cross-culturally. The Japanese, for example, do not expect to display or see displayed negative feelings in facial expressions, and find difficulty in interpreting these when meeting English or American people.

Facial expressions are affected by perspiration of the forehead, blushing, expansion of the eye pupil, tightening of the facial and neck muscles, but most of all changes in the eyebrows and mouth area. Our face comments upon what other people are saying to us and gives them quite powerful feedback. The eyebrows are particularly useful for this. They provide a continuous running commentary, something like the following:

fully raised	—	disbelief
half raised	—	surprise
normal	—	no comment
half lowered	—	puzzled
fully lowered	—	angry

The area round the mouth supplements the work of the eyebrows by expression of pleasure when the mouth is turned up, displeasure when it is turned down. The mouth area also involuntarily displays emotions. We may be tight-lipped when trying to control anger, twitching of the lips or moistening the lips with the tongue when nervous or under strain, full lips pushed well forward when inviting close intimacy, etc.

THE FUNCTIONS OF NON-VERBAL COMMUNICATION

The following are the main functions served by non-verbal communications:

It can support verbal communication. We have already described how gestures can add to or emphasise the words being used, terminal gazes can be used to aid in synchronisation of speech. Tone of voice and facial expression can indicate the mood in which we mean our remarks to be taken — whether serious or light-heartedly for example. The feedback we need when we are speaking on how others are responding so that we can modify our remarks accordingly, is obtained from a variety of non-verbal devices. All these are ways of supporting our verbal communication.

As stated above, it can replace speech, when speech is not possible.

It can perform certain ritualistic functions of everyday life and, in particular, it can communicate complex messages in greetings and farewell ceremonies.

It can express the feelings we have about other people. These will tend to be along the three dimensions of:

Liking or Disliking
Dominant or Submissive Behaviour
Strong or Weak Reaction

This can be expressed diagrammatically in the following way:

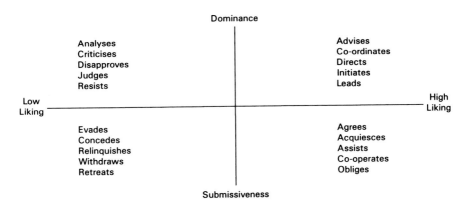

It can be used to express what condition or state of feeling we are in, though we might try to suppress or control this. This is most clearly done by facial expression, though the hands display very well the degree of tension and strength (though not type) of emotion.

It can be used to state how we would like other people to see us, the way we present ourselves for public scrutiny.

WHY BOTHER WITH NON-VERBAL COMMUNICATION

It is fundamental to any attempt to improve our interpersonal skills that we understand what messages are passing between ourselves and others. Non-verbal communication is particularly important to understand because it has such a strong impact. Dr. A. Mehrabian concluded as a result of his researches that of the messages received 7% are verbal, 38% are vocal, and 55% are facial. Michael Argyle suggests that non-verbal messages are sixteen times as strong as verbal ones. Clearly if this is the case, then we need to pay great attention to it.

Furthermore, skill in understanding non-verbal communication enables us to see any disparity between the meaning of the verbal message and the unspoken opinions of the sender. If we develop this skill it enables us to tune into our feelings of discomfort that words we are hearing do not quite ring true.

Thirdly, non-verbal communication tells us about the feelings and emotions of people in a way that verbal utterances very seldom do. This is often the crucial information we need to know.

Finally, we may be able to learn better to control our own non-verbal messages in those situations where this is important. For example, the teacher may well like some of her students and dislike others — she needs to control her non-verbal as well as her verbal behaviour so that such feelings are not apparent. A similar need to control non-verbal messages may be the concern of the host at a party or a counsellor with clients.

FURTHER READING

Three popular books that examine non-verbal behaviour are:

ELKMAN, P. and Frieden, W. **Unmasking the face**. Spectrum, 1975.

FAST, J. **The body language**. Pan Books, 1971. ISBN 0-330-02862-6.

MORRIS, Desmond **Manwatching**. Cape, 1977. ISBN 0-586-04887-1.

For many years, Michael Argyle has been conducting research in this field, and the results of his studies are collected together in:

ARGYLE, Michael **Bodily communication**. Methuen, 1975. ISBN 0-416-55290-0.

Another valuable collection of work by various scholars is:

HINDE, Robert A. ed. **Non-verbal communication**. Cambridge University Press, 1972. ISBN 0-521-08370-2.

A very useful introductory film to the subject is:

Communication: the non-verbal agenda. Produced by Training Films International Ltd, St. Mary's St., Whitchurch, Salop (available for hire).

Chapter 7

The counselling interview

INTRODUCTION
Any person who is responsible for some of the work of other people will find himself every so often needing to engage in a face to face interview with one of them. A part of the manager's job is being responsible for the resolution of problems of substance that face his staff, and some of these can only be resolved by a personal interview session. It follows that if this is a part of his job, it is necessary that he develops the technical and attitudinal skills needed to manage such sessions. Unfortunately the need for such training is hardly recognised in most occupations so there is little willingness or opportunity to undertake formal training. This is the situation generally in colleges of FE. Few heads of department, section heads, librarians, registrars, vice principals or principals have had any formal training in counselling or interviewing and most of them rely on common sense and the experience of having been in charge of men and women over some length of time. Unschooled common sense and experience may work for some teachers in some situations some of the time, but it is a very hit or miss affair and it is difficult to justify such an amateur approach in one of the key areas of management. For it is clear that difficulties in handling the counselling interview or resolving the persistent personnel problems that arise from failure in the interview are among the most worrying problems that managers in colleges face.

The following sections of this chapter are intended to give some help but cannot be expected to replace formal training courses. The purpose of the chapter is to encourage all those involved in the management of people to seek out and undertake some basic training in counselling interviewing.

DEFINITION OF THE AREA
What is it that we are describing as a counselling interview? We can consider three types of interview.

The first is the disciplinary interview in which in one way or another a member of staff has behaved in ways which are not acceptable to the manager. A typical instance might be of a staff member who has persistently failed to be at his classes on time or has failed to keep adequate records of his students' performance. The manager may decide that counselling in any form is inappropriate and that a formal reprimand is required. Given that there is a proven misdemeanour, the situation the principal or head of department organises is a formal one in which hierarchical and judgemental communication is made to the recipient. The manager has the rule book on his side and is making the statement 'You change or else'. It is one-way communication, for the recipient is not required to say anything. Such an interview, one hopes, is rare in FE colleges and managers should do all they can to avoid it. Not only is it destructive of staff relationships and unlikely to increase the motivation of the recipient to do his work well, but it may not even achieve its ostensible purpose. The recipient may well carry on with his unacceptable behaviour but be more careful that it is disguised or covert. However, we have to accept that there are times when every other avenue has been explored and the manager has no choice but to invoke sanctions in a disciplinary interview.

Many matters initially seen as disciplinary by the manager may, however, lead into the second type of interview. This is the appraisal interview in which the staff member and manager explore and analyse job performance in some way or other. The word is not used here in its narrow sense of a formal annual job appraisal as typically described in management literature, but is expanded to include any interview which is looking at how a member of staff is getting along. It would include feedback sessions on new ventures, staff development interviews, the analysis of any kind of apparent blockage in a staff member's work. An interview which is concerned with apparently unsatisfactory performance of some sort or other requires a different approach and is discussed in a later section under the marginal performance interview.

The third type is the personal interview. In this the staff member typically has a problem in his personal life, in his relationships with others, within his own personality, or in his practical circumstances, any of which is seen by him to be affecting his work and life in the college. Whereas the appraisal interview may be initiated either by the manager or the interviewee, the personal interview would commonly be initiated by the interviewee.

In practice, many counselling interviews will contain elements of both types, or may move at stages in the interview from one to another. It is not uncommon for an interview that starts off on a disciplinary point to lead into appraisal and then a discussion of personal problems. In essence, the differences between the two types is very small, and for our purposes we can treat them together. We do not include, however, interviews concerned with staff selection or with technical and administrative matters, neither are we commenting further on the disciplinary interview.

THE OBJECTIVES OF THE INTERVIEW

Interviews commonly go wrong because of a misapprehension of their objective. As a consequence of an interview, if it is initiated by him, the manager hopes for a change in observable behaviour, either in improved skill, greater knowledge, or most commonly in changed attitude, which will enable the staff member not only to deal with the existing problem but also avoid generation of such problems in the future.

The objective of the interview must therefore be to reach a point where the staff member finds a solution acceptable to him, which he sees as his solution to his problem, and which he is committed to implementing. Any solution which is imposed, which is not fully accepted by the staff member, and which is really the solution of the manager, is unlikely to achieve any useful change in behaviour.

It is the inability to keep clear this distinction which makes so many interviews fruitless. Most manager have been trained or have come to accept that in the last resort, and sometimes well before that, it is their decision that has to stand. While there may be many areas of their managerial work where this is a reasonable point of view, it is totally unproductive in the counselling interview. The managerial decision may on the surface be accepted but unless it is internalised by the staff member then it is of no value. For if he does not really accept a decision, he has a hundred ways of preventing it being operated without any open defiance of the management.

THE OVERALL STRATEGY OF THE COUNSELLING INTERVIEW

If we agree that the objective is to find a solution acceptable to the staff member, then the overall strategy of the interview must be to help him explore his own position, to help him define his problem and find a practical course of action to which he is committed and to create the conditions in which this exploration and solution can happen.

It follows that the very last thing a manager should be giving is advice. Advice is totally counter-productive to effective counselling. Advice is a statement of what the solution is for the manager if he were in the problem situation. The objective is not, however, to find solutions for the manager, nor is it to exhibit the superior problem-solving capacity of the manager. Advice is at best irrelevant to the objective, at worst it is the exercise of management power.

We face, however, a considerable problem in implementing this strategy. Teachers find it very difficult not to give advice and exhortation. This, after all, is their training; it has been part of their daily business of being a teacher since they first qualified. However much they may wish to switch their mode of operating in counselling interviews to non-directive facilitating, in practice it generally proves to be too difficult without some formal training. If the college employs a professional counsellor, he or she will have been trained in this skill and can help the teacher or manager to begin acquiring it. But it certainly does not come easily to the average staff member or manager.

To summarise the point of this section:

The strategy of the counselling interview must be to enable the staff member to reach a solution which is his own.

PRECONDITIONS OF THE COUNSELLING INTERVIEW

Counselling interviews, whether of the appraisal or personal type, are only likely to have a successful outcome if certain preconditions are satisfied.

The first and most important of these is the existence of trust between the two people involved. Both must feel confident that the other will not take advantage on another occasion of facts, attitudes, opinions and responses revealed during the interview. Both must therefore believe that the other means well towards him, is concerned with his well-being, does not want to do him down. It is not necessary that the relationship be one of great friendship. It can be entirely neutral in the affective sense, but it must have this level of basic trust. Normally the counselling interview would be bound by the rules of confidentiality on both parties, such that only with the express agreement of the individual should any facts of the interview be passed on to anyone else.

The corollary of the need for trust is that the two people involved must be relatively open with each other. Interviews will only be reasonably successful if openness is seen to be practised by both. One of the commoner causes of abortive interviews is the unwillingness of the interviewee to reveal many of the essential facts of his situation and the failure of the interviewer to encourage or respond to openness. Both are secretive, protective of themselves, disclosing only those parts of themselves which seem safe. This generally arises because of a lack of trust, a suspicion of the other person in this kind of interview. It is understandable enough because the face-to-face situation can be a threatening one to people who are not used to operating on the principle of trust and openness.

The third precondition is the recognition of the equal standing of the other person, a mutual respect of the work of each other and each other's ideas and statements. We cannot deny the existence of different hierarchic ranks or functions but, within the overall acceptance of this, it is important for the manager to recognise the rights of the person he is interviewing, and particularly his right to be seen as equally intelligent, perceptive, motivated and committed. If the unspoken (and possibly subconscious) assumption is that the manager is somehow better endowed with these attributes, then the interview is doomed to failure because it is in effect a reinforcement of the power of the manager to be seen as the superior person. In transactional analysis terms it is the position of 'I'm OK — you're not OK — so you need my help'.

The fourth precondition is that there should be acceptance by both that they may have to change their own attitudes or opinions. The mutual acceptance of changes means that the manager cannot work on the principle that all changes are going to have to be made by the person he is interviewing. Inevitably any period of fruitful interpersonal relationship will be dynamic and reactive and lead to changes and adjustments by both parties, but this process is not always recognised by the manager who may be very resistant to change in himself while encouraging a great deal of change in the interviewee. On occasions it may be that after discussion of a problem it is the manager who needs to make changes himself and the staff member to remain as he is.

The fifth precondition is that the manager should not bring into the meeting any strong feelings of anger, hostility or the like. Very strong negative emotional reactions will make any constructive work towards a solution very difficult. Such a situation most commonly arises in the disciplinary interview, although by no means confined to that, and it may be sparked off by the specific circumstances that have occasioned the interview or be a reflection of a longer term feeling of anger or hostility. In transactional analysis terms, this is the 'Not OK Child' of the manager taking charge and it clearly makes a counselling interview impossible. It is important that the manager creates an atmosphere of support and warmth.

To summarise the above points, we have suggested that the essential preconditions for a successful counselling session are:

The existence of trust
Openness
Recognition of equal standing and mutual respect
Mutual acceptance of change
Avoidance of strong emotional feelings

THE COUNSELLING INTERVIEW

We can divide our consideration of the counselling interview into setting and process. The setting is the background or scenery against which the events happen and the process is the activity of the two participants against this background.

The Setting. We have only to recall the rooms of a number of college principals or heads of department to observe how different they are in appearance. If we have a room of our own we arrange it to reflect an image of ourselves, an image presumably reflecting how we want to be seen publicly in our function as the holder of a particular job. There are no rules about how we should or should not arrange our rooms. Some may like a room with a clear desk and tidy appearance, others prefer to have one with work in various stages scattered on every available surface. Some like to fill walls with charts and diagrams, others like blank walls, still others like their own personal choice of pictures or posters. Some have nothing in the office that does not reflect their job, others let all sorts of interests from their private life intrude such as family photographs, golf clubs, etc. Some spend care in arranging their room with aesthetic sensitivity and do not have an ugly object or discordant colour in sight; others pay no attention to the aesthetic appearance at all.

In one sense none of this matters: it is entirely up to the room occupant to express himself as he thinks fit. But in the counselling situation it is going to make some difference. From the perspective of a staff member coming into a room to discuss some sensitive matter, the clues he picks up from the appearance of the room are a part of the communication process in the counselling interview. We are all aware that different rooms have different feelings or atmospheres — some seem relaxing, others impersonal, messy, forbidding, cold, efficient, etc. If staff members react badly to the atmosphere of the room, they may interpret the clues given out as statements about the manager's attitude. We cannot argue that the manager should arrange his room solely to get the maximum benefit from a counselling interview; after all he uses his room for many other purposes. He might give some thought, however, to the likely effects on the people who enter his room and consider whether he wants to make some changes in its appearance.

Some changes are very easy because they are concerned with non-permanent phenomena. The two most obvious of these are the positioning of chairs and the dress of the interviewer. In most rooms the occupant has a number of choices of where he places his own and the visitor's chair for a counselling interview. He may take the typical manager's position behind the desk with the other chair in front of it. He may sit behind the desk but turn sideways to a chair brought in at the side of the desk. He may have a larger chair than his visitor, a more comfortable chair or a higher chair.

Whatever decision the manager makes, we would suggest it is done with some consideration of the likely effect. Generally his decision is likely to be based on the degree of distance or closeness he wishes to establish and the degree of dominance or equality he wishes to work in. In a similar way, the manner in which the interviewer dresses gives some clues about distance and formality and there is no doubt that people respond in different and subjective ways to the way people dress. We are not of course suggesting that managers try to dress to suit the interviewee, or have one suit for discipline interviews and another for personal interviews. They should, however, at least be aware of the possible effects of all parts of the setting of the interview and that must include their dress. If a manager is failing to generate the relaxed atmosphere or degree of warmth or empathy he is aiming at he might consider, among other things, the effect of his own appearance.

The Process. No one can be sure before an interview starts how it will proceed. The process is reactive. But the manager can work with some clear guidelines within which the interaction will flow. We suggest that he might take account of the following rules.

The first of these is that the interview should be free from interruption. If someone comes in through the door or the telephone rings, it is never possible to get back exactly to the point the interview was at. Something is always lost and it may be very difficult for the interviewee, painfully working through a problem, to get back onto his line of thought and feeling. Furthermore, it is an indication that the manager cannot or will not give one hundred per cent of his time and attention to the staff member's problem. So doors should be firmly barred and telephone temporarily cut off.

Secondly, the atmosphere of the interview will be set by the manner in which the staff member is greeted. Michael Argyle in his work on interpersonal behaviour has reported on the effect of various methods of entry into offices, forms of greeting and movements by the incumbent. The manager who keeps someone waiting in front of his desk while he finishes some work is clearly asserting dominance but is not setting up the atmosphere for a successful counselling interview. Hopefully, he will smile and greet the entrant with an initial tone of voice that expresses non-possessive warmth. He will have to decide whether to rise, to walk round the desk to the entrant, to meet him at the door, to shake hands, to go through various conventions of greeting and ice-breaking. The major point is that the entrant should not feel worse by the time the interview proper starts than he did when he first came through the door.

The purpose of all subsequent transactions must be to switch, in transactional analysis terms, to an Adult to Adult exchange. If the staff member is very upset he may be looking for a Child — Nurturing Parent transaction; if he is very angry he may be looking for a Child — Child transaction (in other words a slanging match); if he is apprehensive at being found fault with, he may be expecting a Child — Critical Parent transaction. But whatever the expectation and the initial exchange, the manager must switch to the Adult — Adult transactions as soon as possible, because only then can reality problems and solutions begin to be explored. One of the problems for the manager is that he might easily find himself hooked into a Nurturing or Critical Parent or into his Angry Child, and indeed might even start the interview in that state so that he was preventing the staff member from staying in his Adult state. If, however, the manager insists on making Adult responses, in the end he will switch the interviewee into his Adult as well. It is essential to do this because only if solutions are accepted by the interviewee in his Adult state is he likely to implement them after he has left the office. If he accepts solutions in his Child state ('I must do what the boss says') or his Parent state ('That is what I ought to do') then it is very likely he will not implement the solution. This is a hard task for the manager. To stay in the Adult state against pressure to move from it requires some determination and strength of will.

Operating within this kind of transaction, the manager will need to spend much of his time listening. With only occasional prompting or facilitating he will let the staff member work through the situation, identify the problem and search for solutions. Listening, however, is a difficult skill which most of us lack. We normally do a rough scan of what we are hearing so that we get the general sense, but our mind is also dealing with other matters as well. Other thoughts keep on breaking into our mind, and other stimuli keep on catching our attention. We look out of the window, or at the half-read report on our desk, or begin to think about the next interview we have when this one is finished. Listening with full concentration so that we catch all the nuances and unspoken comments, the non-verbal signs which suggest that something is still hidden, is very hard and requires practice. It is also a very positive act, because the act of concentrated listening conveys the message to the speaker that the listener cares, is prepared to give time and effort, respects what he has to say and wants to hear it. Conversely, casual scanning by the listener, accompanied by fidgeting, looking out of the window, or at the ceiling, prowling round the room, picking up or putting down objects, and a bored or faraway look, tells the speaker that the listener does not really care or value what he has to say, or is prepared to put in much effort. It follows that the positive act of listening must be accompanied by some obvious non-verbal signs — for example of sitting alertly, looking at the speaker and showing an expression of interest and sympathy. We can portray the listening process in the following way:

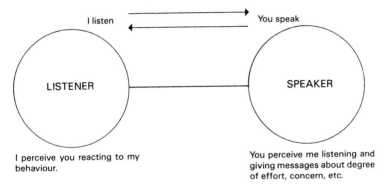

The following is a check list of behaviours which will aid or hinder effective listening.

DON'T	DO
Let your mind wander on to other things.	Give total concentration to the speaker.
Let your eyes wander from the speaker or give other physical signs that you are not attending.	Do look at the speaker and give full physical attention.
Sit (or stand) in a posture expressing apathy, impatience, or other negative states.	Do assume a posture which shows interest in the speaker.
Think of what you want to say next while she is speaking.	Give full attention of your mind to what is being said.
Give indications by gesture, facial expressions or comment of whether you agree or not with what is being said.	Accept everything that is said without comment, either verbal or non-verbal.
Look cold, reserved or hostile.	Look warm and concerned.

DON'T	**DO**
Avoid all verbal utterance of encouragement (unless you are skilled at giving it non-verbally).	Give verbal signs of encouragement (or non-verbal signs if you are skilful at this).
Interrupt if the speaker pauses for a minute.	Tolerate silences.
Give an impression of heaviness, or seriousness or intensity.	Give a relaxed impression, with humour where appropriate.
Start listening with pre-conceived ideas about the message or the person.	Come in with a totally open mind.
Concentrate only on the voice of the speaker.	Observe the non-verbal statement of the speaker.

The manager will, of course, also be making his own contributions as well as listening, and the amount of this will vary according to the type and circumstances of the interview. We are suggesting that the primary purpose of interventions of the manager is to help the staff member identify problems and find acceptable solutions. The most useful way in which a manager can help in this is:

Firstly, to lead the staff member through an analysis of the problem as stated to a redefinition of the problem (not, of course, by stating what the 'real' problem is);

Secondly, to present useful relevant information;

Thirdly, to lead him to formulate alternative lines of action (not to state what the alternatives are);

Fourthly, to present fact-based estimates of the consequences of the various lines of action;

Fifthly, to lead him to formulate the lines of action he proposes to follow, and to note both their mutual commitments in this.

The problem for the manager in making interventions, apart from having the skill to respond rapidly with useful statements when the time is right, is to avoid satisfying his own needs for interaction with another person by airing his prejudices, expressing his feelings, making debating points, scoring off the other person, reminiscing, or working out arguments and solutions.

He will certainly have to satisfy these needs at various times, but not during the counselling interview.

Inevitably, no respondent can avoid getting involved to some extent in the dialogue, and each individual will bring in elements of his own style. One way of thinking of these differences of response style is to categorise them into the following:

The non-committal
The interpretative
The probing
The supporting
The evaluating

Supposing that a staff member, in discussing his future, said:

> 'I thought I better tell you — I have had this very good offer of a job back in my old firm. I thought a lot about it but I've decided I would rather stay and make my future in the college. So I will be working for promotion in the department.'

If we suppose that the staff member in the considered view of the head of department is not a particularly strong prospect for promotion — in fact is just about adequate in his present job — how might he respond?

The **supportive** response might be:
'Good. I'm glad you've made up your mind where you want to go. I'll be all the help I can in your career, though the promotion race is tough nowadays. If you run across any difficulties you want to talk out I'm always here and if you don't get the promotion you want we will find other ways to help.'
(Whatever you decide, I'll make helpful noises.)

The **evaluative** response might be:
'I guess that if you weigh up the pros and cons you are probably doing the best thing for your future.'
(I'll tell you whether you've got it right or wrong.)

The **probing** response might be:
'I wonder if you have really thought through the policy of promotion in the college. How do you match up to the possibilities?'
(You have got some thinking to do.)

The **interpretative** response might be:
'What you seem to have decided is to go for safety and the familiar work, rather than the challenges and dangers of an unpredictable future.'
(I will tell you what you were thinking.)

The **non-committal** approach might be:
'You seem to be saying that you see future promotion prospects best in this college.'
(Tell me again what you are saying.)

There are times in any interview when we need elements of all five responses but it is possible that most of us will tend to lapse into our favourite and habitual style, however inappropriate it is. Accepting that elements of all styles are needed, we would argue that the uncommitted response is of particular value. The act of feeding back to the interviewee what he appears to be saying has proved a very effective device for enabling him to analyse his situation.

We do not want to argue that the manager must avoid all expression of warmth just because we are suggesting that his major activity will be positive listening, providing of facts and uncommitted responses of feeding back what has been said. Indeed one of the key elements in successful counselling appears to be the establishment of empathy. Obviously there must be a relationship between the manager and the staff member for anything to happen at all. Sympathy or pity or possessive warmth are unhelpful. Empathy is perhaps best defined as the acceptance by the interviewee that the interviewer understands his feelings or is trying to do so, without making any demands from that knowledge. It requires suspension of concern with one's own needs, feelings and thoughts, to concentrate on being with the needs, feelings and thoughts of the other.

In relation to empathy and most of the other points we have made, the part of non-verbal behaviour is crucial. All the small signs and gestures of our facial muscles, hands and bodies either reinforce or destroy the effect we are trying to make. The skilful interviewer has to acquire control of his non-verbal behaviour.

The final point to make is that although we have referred several times to defining the problem and then finding a solution, there are many situations where there is no apparent solution. The problem and the situation may be unalterable, but the value of the counselling interview is that the staff member's perception of his situation may be changed. To come to a realistic understanding of his situation may be the first step to moving from a distorted view to a tolerance of the situation and its accompanying pressures and stresses. So it would be a mistake to strain after a solution at all costs or regard the exercise as a failure if a solution does not emerge.

SOME COMMON TRAPS

The counselling interview is bedevilled with traps. It is not only the unexperienced and unwary but on occasions the skilled counsellor who falls headlong into the pit. No one is likely to conduct the perfect interview. What we need to do is to avoid the traps as often as we can and learn from our mistakes. The following list of pitfalls is taken from the work of Jean Brookes, a teacher of counselling skills at Thameside College of Technology.

1. Excessive curiosity which leads the manager to asking too many questions and constantly leads her off on the wrong track.
2. Too much haste to find a quick solution to the presented problem. This fails to solve or even to notice the real problem which underlies the problem initially presented.
3. Blocking the client's expression of feelings and emotions. Trying to stop him crying or expressing his distress doesn't help in any way.
4. Being too busy to listen. This is the ultimate put-down for a client who may have invested much courage in approaching the manager and asking for some of her time.
5. Filling silences. If the manager cannot tolerate silence and jumps in with questions or comments whenever they occur, the real issues will never be reached.
6. Being a clever psychologist. Some managers fancy themselves as amateur psychologists and believe they are particularly perceptive. They off-load their insights on to the staff member whom they are trying to help.
7. Wanting to be liked. Some managers have a desperate need to be indispensable and it is more important to them that the client likes them than that he is helped.
8. Wanting to take over the client's problems and solve them. The manager can want to do too much and not accept the client as a grown person who can take responsibility for himself.

9. Imposing one's own values on the client. The manager may communicate her own set of values and recipes for life, which are different from and perhaps antagonistic to those of the client.

10. Identifying with the client and his problems, but in so doing imposing her own experiences in the belief that common experience creates sympathy.

Our own anxieties cause us to fall into these traps. The problems a member of staff brings to us, and his comments on them, may create considerable stress or unease in us. Sometimes they are too close to home for comfort. All we can do is be aware of the traps and avoid them the best we can. Fore knowledge is a powerful weapon.

CONCLUSION

We can summarise much of what has been said in this paper in the following tabular form:

Counselling interviews should be:	Counselling interviews should not be:
Necessary	Ritualistic
Open to change	Closed to change
Trusting	Distrusting
Descriptive	Evaluative
Adult-Adult	Parent or Child
Positive	Negative
Building	Destroying
Accepting	Rejecting
Listening	Telling
Together	Apart
Respecting	Condescending

It is unlikely that all those in management positions will be able to become trained in counselling skills. Many will see formal training as a low priority among the many calls on their time. For those who do desire some professional help, there are, in most areas, short courses which will help to improve the manager's skill without committing him to large investments of time or full professional training. If the college or the local polytechnic has a team of fully qualified counsellors, they can provide expert help and advice to managers as required.

If, however, the manager is not able or is unwilling to take part in any kind of training, however brief, then a careful study of the points made in this paper may help him to improve his technique in interviews with his staff.

FURTHER READING

Most books on counselling are written for those who are professional counsellors or are in training. Furthermore most are concerned with counselling students in a school setting. One exception to this, and an excellent introduction to counselling and guidance, is:

MILLER, John C. **Tutoring. The guidance & counselling role of the tutor in vocational preparation.** Further Education Curriculum Review and Development Unit, DES, 1982. ISBN 0-85522-100-3.

Two useful books which serve as general introductions to counselling are:

SPERRY, Len and Hess, L. R. **Contact counselling. Communications skills for people in organisations.** Addison-Wesley, 1974. ISBN 0-201-07116-9.

This is a valuable book to work through with a great deal of practical material, exercises, and cases. It focuses on the manager in the organisation and uses a transactional analysis background.

WYMOT, William. **Dyadic communication: a transactional perspective.** Addison-Wesley, 1975. ISBN 0-201-08615-8.

This is a useful book which concentrates on what happens between two people when they relate and has many points of value to conducting a counselling interview. There is a useful table of helpful and unhelpful actions on page 82 in the following text on self-development for managers.

BURGOYNE, John C., Boydell, Tom and Pedler, Mike. **Self-development.** Association of Teachers of Management, 1978.
from: The Association of Teachers of Management,
       Polytechnic of Central London,
       35 Marylebone Road,
       LONDON NW1 5LS.

For those who wish to study counselling in greater depth, we recommend the following two books which have had great influence in the development of counsellor training in this country.

HALMOS, Paul. **The faith of the counsellors.** Constable, rev. ed., 1977. ISBN 0-09-462110-1.

ROGERS, Carl R. **Client-centred therapy.** Constable, 1951. ISBN 0-09-453990-1.

A recent valuable guide is the following:

BOARD, Robert de **Counselling people at work.** Gower, 1983. ISBN 0-566-02376-8.

Chapter 8

The counselling interview for marginal performance

This chapter is based on material by Russ Curtis, former Associate Tutor at the Further Education Staff College

Part of our job as managers is to help those for whom we are responsible perform, at the very least, at a minimally satisfactory level. For many of our colleagues that is not a problem. They do their job well and never cause us any concern.

There are two categories of people who will worry us. Firstly, there is a very small percentage of people in every organisation who are totally impossible in their behaviour or their work output or both. The organisation does not know what to do with them, no actions taken ever seem to resolve the problem, and they are a general nuisance all round. Marginal performance interviewing, however well it is done, will have no effect on such people. The organisation has only two choices: to get rid of them or put up with them. A manager should avoid spending too much time on such people, because it is almost certain to be wasted.

It is another matter however with the second category of people. They may form up to 30 per cent of the work force and are distinguished by two characteristics. They clearly have the capacity to work at satisfactory levels of performance yet they intermittently or constantly fail to reach such levels in important areas of their work. It is with these staff that the manager can concentrate his activity and skills in marginal performance interviewing with reasonable hope of seeing some improvement.

The manager must make two assumptions:

1. All human behaviour is caused; it is not random. People behave the way they do because it makes sense of them, however inconvenient it may be for others and however bizarre it may seem.
2. Marginal performance has many causes, many of which do not lie with the employee himself. It is more likely than not, if an employee is behaving in a way that management find unsatisfactory, that the causes lie with the manager or some external factor rather than with the employee. It is crucial that such an assumption is made if a subsequent interview is not to dissolve into mutual recriminations.

CAUSES OF MARGINAL PERFORMANCE

1. **Managerial causes**
   The management selected a candidate for a job which he is not fully equipped to do. The management selected or promoted a candidate to a job and then took insufficient care with his induction.

The work a teacher is being asked to do is not related to his skills and expertise, though he is capable of performing it. For example, a teacher of high-level electronics may be asked to teach basic mathematics.

The work of a teacher may be changed from that which he does well and finds rewarding to work in which he has little interest.

The work of a teacher may be changed to something very novel and no staff training or development programme made available to enable him to cope with it.

Promotions to supervisory and management positions may have been given to teachers who have no skills in those areas. Their poor management performance invites marginal responses from the staff they supervise.

2. External causes

If the labour market is static, the employee cannot easily leave his job. If he has cause for dissatisfaction, but no way of resolving it, he is likely to perform his duties less well.

Family and social relationships affect job performance. As such relationships are generally becoming more fluid and complex, temporary or permanent effects on staff may become more common.

Political, cultural and social mores change but organisations sometimes hang on to a world that has disappeared. If employees see a disjunction between the world external to the organisation and its internal life, this can lead to marginal performance.

3. Employee causes

The employee may for a variety of reasons be unwilling to work at or above a minimally acceptable level.

The employee may perform marginally because of factors affecting his physical and mental health.

The employee may be unable or unwilling to operate within the social network of the organisation. He may not deal satisfactorily with people and be so inept in interpersonal relationships that reasonable decisions cannot easily take place with him.

THE INTERVIEW

The manager has a duty, whatever the cause, to persuade his staff to improve on marginal or unsatisfactory performance. Let us consider two situations.

The head of department, as manager, hears that a lecturer has been turning up late for his classes over the last fortnight. He also receives a complaint from a training officer of a firm that his employees are not being taught the agreed syllabus on their day in the college. Both teachers are relatively competent. Neither falls into the category of hopeless cases. What does the head of department do? If, as seems likely, he sends for them so that he can sort out what is wrong and what should be done, he is about to engage in a marginal performance interview. Such an interview requires some level of skill and a clear strategy if there is to be a constructive outcome. The following is suggested as a model.

Setting up the interview

A firm arrangement needs to be made when both head and lecturer are free for at least one hour. There should be no disturbance during the interview. A private room with an 'engaged' sign on the door and the telephone off the hook is essential.

THE OPENING DISCUSSION

The purpose of the opening discussion is to enable the lecturer and head of department to reach a mutually agreed definition of the problem. This part of the discussion has to be handled skilfully. If it goes wrong the interview is seldom recoverable and subsequent steps are largely a waste of time.

Step One

Greeting. This should be friendly but brief. No irrelevant material should be introduced. It is a mistake to set the lecturer at his ease by asking how the job is going or how his family is getting on. The lecturer's response can throw the whole subsequent interview. Also, if the manager gives some praise before outlining the symptoms of poor performance, it will simply confuse the discussion. The interview can start by a very simple set of statements.

'Oh hello, Joe, thank you for coming. Do come and sit down.'

Step Two

Statement of the Symptoms. This should be a simple statement of the reason for the discussion. The head offers the information not as undisputed t ruth but as what he has been led to believe. He can be tentative, though he will presumably have checked beforehand as well as he can. Thus he might say, 'It seems you have been late for your classes every morning this week,' or 'I have a letter from Mr. Young complaining you are not teaching the agreed syllabus to his apprentices.'

If the manager's information is wrong and the lecturer can convince him, the interview is over. If there is a dispute between his assertion and the head's information, the manager should break off the interview and check his evidence. There is a general rule that applies throughout all stages of the interview: if at any time either of the participants becomes over-emotional, the interview should be terminated for the time being. No useful discussion can take place in a cauldron of seething emotion.

Step Three

Defining the problem. This is a crucial stage of the interview for the HoD is seeking an operable definition of the problem, and whatever the lecturer comes up with will determine what follows. The lead-in question is simply put.

'What is the problem?'

It is almost certain that the manager will want to ask probing or clarifying questions following the answer, but if the manager feels the lecturer is playing a game with him, for example by raising old injustices as an excuse for present failings or scapegoating some other colleague or organisation, the subsequent questions will expose this and the lecturer will be brought back to consider the question again:

'What is the problem?'

If the lecturer seems stuck and unable to define the problem behind the stated symptoms, the manager might raise the following problem areas.
Is it to do with your working conditions?

> with equipment or supplies?
> with any of the systems or procedures?
> with the behaviour of other staff?
> with the load of work?
> with the pace of work?
> with actions by supervisors or managers?
> with a problem you have yourself?
> with lack of information?
> with lack of training facilities?

And he must always ask the question:

> 'Am I the problem?'

Step Four
Other factors. A standard clarifying question must be asked at this stage.

> 'What other factors might be affecting the situation?'

The lecturer must be given every opportunity to sound out the problem definition and add to what he has already given as the major problem. Marginal performance is seldom caused by a single factor. To address only the major cause without considering other contributing factors will not likely lead to a complete solution.

Step Five
The real problem. The manager reflects back the lecturer's definition of the problem, and repeats it in various forms until both are satisfied. There may be a need for more clarifying and probing questions until the manager has got it right. This step concludes the opening discussion. The manager has done no more than state the symptoms and then asked questions.

He has made no value judgements, offered no advice, suggested no solutions. What he has ended up with is a clear definition of the problem.

THE MIDDLE DISCUSSION
The purpose of this part of the interview is to help the lecturer consider various solutions to the problem and to commit himself to one of them. The sequence of steps will often need to be repeated several times as a solution-searching loop before the lecturer commits himself to an action. It is unlikely to be such a tidy pattern of interaction as the following sequence of steps may suggest.

Step One
Solution-seeking. Having defined the problem, the lecturer is now asked to suggest a solution to it.

> 'What can you do about it?'

The manager may need to be persistent in pinning the lecturer to an answer. A common strategy of the lecturer will be evasion, silence, or apparent impotence. 'I can't think of anything that will help.' The manager must clearly try to avoid suggesting solutions except as a last resort. If the solution is not one initiated by the lecturer he is less likely to be committed to it, but some prompting might be necessary in some cases.

Step Two
Assessing the solution. 'Will that solve the problem?' If the answer is no, the discussion has to return to step one and another more practical solution found. In practice, steps one and two will often merge into each other as successive solutions are checked and found wanting. The purpose of step two is not only to make sure that there is a practical way forward, but to gain some commitment to the solution.

Step Three
Other helpful actions. 'What else could be done?' This question is asked so that the lecturer has the opportunity to flush out the solution. There may be some relatively small and easy action which would help him and can be agreed and attached to the solution.

Step Four
Firming up on the solution. At this stage a clear statement of the proposed solution needs to be agreed as a summary of the preceeding three steps. The lead statement is — 'then the best solution is . . .'

Step Five
Feasibility of the solution. 'Can you do it?' It is essential that the interviewer confirms that the lecturer will be able to carry out the proposed action. It is common enough to arrive at a good solution in discussion, which then turns out to be one which is impracticable, at least for the persons concerned. If that is the case, the interview has to revert to step one of the middle section, 'What can you do about it?' If however the performer feels he can do it, then his agreement at this point confirms him commitment to execute the solution.

Step Six
Date of initiation. 'How long will it take?' The interviewer carries on with his technique of pinning the lecturer to specific actions by direct questions. The middle discussion is concluded by setting the solution in a time framework which further commits the lecturer to carry it out.

THE END DISCUSSION
The end discussion is a recapitulation of the areas of agreement which leaves no room for ambiguity or differences of interpretation. This recapitulation should be agreed in writing and can then be concluded in a friendly manner.

Step One
Recapitulation. So the problem is . . . The solution is . . . and you will carry it out by . . .

Step Two
Record. 'This written record of our agreement is confirmed as accurate by both of us.'

Step Three
Closing the interview. The interview can be concluded by some expression of confidence in the lecturer by the manager, and his belief that there will be a successful outcome to the problem. He should then thank the lecturer for his time and co-operation.

Step Four
Reviewing performance. Before the manager turns to other business, it is very useful if he reviews critically his performance and commits his thoughts to paper. Marginal performance interviewing is full of traps and skill is acquired by reflecting on hard-won experience.

Postscript
The skills required in interviewing, as distinct from the strategy employed, are those we have already described in the chapter on the counselling interview. The first of these is that of active listening but also of great importance is the control of non-verbal behaviour and the creation of an empathetic and trusting environment.

In this section we have concentrated on strategy rather than skills because a sound strategy by the manager in this kind of interview minimises the risk that he will come to grief. It helps to keep to a simple plan and follow through the script.

Complexity, elaboration, ambiguity and uncertainty create very high demands for skill and perception. In fluid situations with no clear strategy or scripts, the procedure becomes, in Russ Curtis' words, 'extemporaneous theatre'. Simple though the script is, it offers the manager a fair chance of manoeuvring the lecturer to acknowledge his problem, search for and find a workable solution and commit himself to it within a stable timescale.

FURTHER READING
Various approaches other than the one outlined here are described in:

CURTIS, Russ. **Management of marginal and unsatisfactory performance.** Part I: Introduction (Information bank paper; 1700), Coombe Lodge, 1982.
STEWART, Valerie and STEWART, Andrew. **Managing the poor performer.** Gower, 1983. ISBN 0-566-02248-6.

Chapter 9

Whose problem is it?

A crucial question in all relationships is:

'How do I decide that something is wrong and that I ought to do something about it?'

This might seem a matter of common sense but it raises a very fundamental issue: when have I got a problem, and if I have one is it really mine or is it someone else's? The ownership of problems needs to be clearly established in order to determine appropriate behaviour. The reason this is not simply a matter of common sense is that it is in the interests of many people to push their problem towards us and encourage us to own it as ours. It is our predeliction to accept other people's problems as ours and then engage in all sorts of complex and sometimes painful activity to cope with 'our' problem.

Helen Clinard has suggested one way of establishing the ownership and nature of problems. Taking the focus as the individual we examine how you, as an individual, see the behaviour of other people. The first question you ask about any particular piece of behaviour is:

1. 'Is it something I appreciate or not?'

If it is something appreciated, then the appropriate behaviour is expressing that appreciation or giving positive reinforcement in some appropriate way. If it is not appreciated, the second question is:

2. 'Is it causing a problem or not?'

If it is not causing a problem there is no need to respond to it in any way. If it is causing a problem, then the next three questions aim to locate the ownership of the problem.

3. 'Is it causing me a problem?' or
4. 'Is it causing him a problem?' or
5. 'Is it causing both of us a problem?'

It is critical that we think very carefully about the answers to each of these questions, for on their answsers depends the next course of action.

1. **If he has the problem,** then you have a choice. You have no obligation whatsoever to help other people with their problems unless you are paid to do so. If you do decide of your free will to help someone with a problem, then the basis of that help must be to facilitate him finding his solution to his problem, and this is best achieved through counselling techniques. At no stage should you take on the problem as though it were yours, however much your own sympathetic feelings allied with manipulation by the owner of the problem will push you towards such an action. You have the right, and it would be perfectly proper to exercise it, to say 'that is your problem,' and

leave. That is of course easier said to a comparative stranger than to the person closest to you.

2. **If you have the problem,** then you have four possible choices. You can change yourself

   You can change the person responsible for the behaviour
   You can change your environment
   You can decide to live with the problem and take no action. Note that this is not the same as doing nothing. It is a positive decision.

3. In making these decisions you need to ask one further question about the behaviours which cause you a problem. Are the behaviours creating a problem which has a tangible or concrete effect on me? Or are they creating a problem for me because they affect my feelings or go against my values?
   If the problem is a tangible one then you can deal with it through one of the four choices indicated above, but if it arises from a conflict of values then, although the four choices are still valid, a prime requirement is to discuss, consult and exchange views with the other person on a difference of values or the nature of the feeling response.

4. **If we both have the problem,** then the choices available are:
   For both of us to decide to live with the problem;
   For either one of us to deal with our part of the problem by one of the methods described in 2, above;
   For both of us to engage in mutual problem solving. This will most probably involve us in a rational assessment of options in terms of solutions related to desired outcomes and personal costs and investments.

A decision on ownership of the problem is a critical one and it is important that what is being said here is clearly understood. The problem is owned by the person who is initially bothered or concerned about the situation. It is he who defines it as a problem. The person who is the cause may not feel there is a problem, and even if he does he may have no concern to do anything about it. Ownership of the problem is not about responsibility for, or cause of, but concern about the situation. The person who owns the problem is the person who wants a change, not necessarily the person who needs to change.

In situations where people are working together, one person's identification of his problem may quickly lead to a mutual ownership of the problem by those involved. Where one person identifies his problem and wants a change it does not necessarily become a mutual problem, but it does not mean either than the other people can ignore it. In many practical situations their co-operation in helping him change the situation is something one should reasonably expect, and in some cases it is essential. The value of identifying problem ownership is as a device which helps us choose the most appropriate ways of responding.

Some practical examples

Let us consider the problems of a lecturer (A) and his head of department (B). The lecturer has the following problems:

He feels inadequate to teach some of the new work in a course for unemployed youths which is shortly to start.

He is angry with one of the technicians who, he claims, will not co-operate in providing some audio-visual equipment.

He is annoyed because he has been given a heavier teaching load than other lecturers.

He is critical of the general lack of effort displayed by section heads in his department.

These are not B's problems. They are problems defined by A which (a) cause him concern and (b) which can be described in terms of actions or activities. A feels angry, annoyed, inadequate and critical. His feelings directly relate to new work he has been given, the actions of a technician, the allocation of comparative work loads, and the behaviour of his section head. They are his problems because he has identified them and it is he who wants a change. This is true in spite of the fact that they are mainly caused by other people's failings.

The head of department (B) has the following problems:

He is worried about specific failures by A to teach a syllabus as instructed.

He is anxious in case the principal criticises the poor student exam results which might occur on A's course.

He is puzzled about how to find a replacement from the rest of the staff to take over some of A's work.

Although these problems concern A, they are not his problems. It is the head of department (B) who feels worried, anxious and puzzled and who wants to make changes.

What can A do about his problems? The choices are to change himself, to change others, to change the environment or to live with the situation.

Change himself: He could develop skills to teach the new work demanded of him. He could change his attitude so that he did not care even if his performance was not very good. He could decide to cope with the heavy work load or reduce his commitments to each bit of it so as to reduce his energy input overall. He could do without his audio-visual equipment or set it up himself. he could close his mind to the failures of his section heads.

These kinds of strategies require a mixture of changed activities and changed attitudes in relation to work.

Change others: He could persuade his head of department to reduce his work-load and reallocate to other staff the courses which cause him most distress. He could persuade the technician to co-operate with him or make a formal complaint that might result in the technician reassessing his behaviour. He could induce the section heads over whom he had any influence to view their job more responsibly.

This range of responses requires from A some constructive confrontation activity with associated persuading and negotiating skills.

Change the environment: He could leave his job, ask for a transfer into another department or into a different kind of post in the college. He could change his informal contacts among the staff. He could encourage a change in the structure of the organisation — for example from section heads to short-term project teams.

Some of these activities are within his immediate power and require a reassessment of life or career plans; others require the co-operation of other people and would take time to implement. The head of department can offer counselling help to the lecturer, provided that he does not also define the situations as his problem.

Let us now consider a problem that is jointly owned by A and B, the lecturer and the head of department.

The lecturer cannot get enthusiastic about much of his work programme and is concerned that his work is not of high standard. The head of department feels it is his job to keep his staff motivated and he is concerned about the indifferent quality of much of the lecturer's teaching. Both are dealing with the same problem: A's lack of enthusiasm and consequent low standard of performance. Both feel concern and both want changes though their initial positions for solving the problem are different. A wants B to give him alternative programmes of work; B wants A to put more effort into his existing programme.

Mutual problem-solving can be initiated by a brain-storming session when all possible solutions, however improbable, are laid on the table. The key to successful brain-storming is the total suppression of critical reaction to suggestions either by the proposer or the receiver and, as a corollary to that, an absence of any emotional reaction — scorn, anxiety, etc. Once all the possible solutions are on the table each solution can be analysed in terms of its practicability, cost and consequences for each partner, and the best workable compromise reached.

It will not be every day that a neat solution is available which will cope with all the problems of both partners. There will often be a 'more or less' solution in which, for example, the HoD accepts that he will have to tolerate a lower level of enthusiasm in his staff than he would deem appropriate, and the lecturer accepts that he will have to work a bit harder on the courses he does not like, but some shift can be made in his timetable to give him some work that excites him more and further changes can be offered for consideration at a named date in the future. An alternative approach is to adopt the marginal performance interview as a script for mutual problem-solving. Instead of addressing each question in the script to one person, it is addressed to both.

SUMMARY

1. A key skill in interpersonal relations is the identification of the owner of the problem.
1. Ownership is held by the person who is worried by the situation, not necessarily the person who causes the problem.
3. There will always be a tendency for problem owners to manipulate others into feeling that they also have the problem. Very often people are willing accomplices in this shift.
4. The location of ownership determines the approach in any subsequent interaction. Different skills are required for different situations of ownership.

Chapter 10

Groups in organisations

Whenever people gather together in an organisation to engage in mutual consideration of work problems, a group has formed and a meeting is taking place. Whether the outcome of that interaction is productive depends not only on the skill of the individuals in conducting their business, not only on their capacity to think up bright and imaginative ideas that will aid in the solution of their problems, but also at a more basic level — on their clear understanding of the purposes and functions of the meeting.

One common reason for the unsatisfactory outcome of a meeting, with members frustrated and problems unresolved, is a confusion among the members of the purposes for which the meeting was called and the function it was serving. Although a meeting can serve more than one purpose at the same time and may in the course of a session move from one kind of assembly to another, members will experience considerable difficulty if they are not clear at any one time what kind of meeting they are in. Expectations can then be unrealistic, behaviour can be inappropriate, and interest can evaporate.

Any categorisation over-simplifies and in presenting the following typology based on differing purpose and function, I am aware that there may be meetings which do not fall easily into any of the categories. My purpose is to sharpen awareness of the different kinds of meetings, as a step towards improving individual and team skills for the accomplishment of the purposes for which people have joined together.

A TYPOLOGY OF MEETINGS

1. **A Command Meeting**

   This is a meeting called by a manager to instruct his subordinates to undertake certain tasks, or to lay down rules for future behaviour. Members may ask questions and seek clarification, but they are not there to offer their own ideas or comment on those given. The manager, in the military style of the commander, exerts total control over the meeting. His contributions are directive, and to a lesser extent prescriptive. A command meeting is appropriate if the members are prepared to accept the manager's authority without question and to carry out his commands. If they are not, it will either be abortive in that its decisions will be ignored or it will turn into a conflict meeting with the authority of the manager in dispute.

2. **Ritual meetings**

   One of the functions of meetings is to reinforce the bonds of attachment members feel towards the organisation and to handle critical periods when organisational membership is at issue. There are therefore meetings whose purpose is to initiate people into membership of the organisation or one of its sub-groups; there are meetings to mark the departure of people from the organisation or sub-group; there are meetings to mark the opening or the closure of the organisation itself. There are meetings whose function is to reaffirm the identity of the organisation or sub-group and re-establish group membership identities. Such, for example, is the symbolic purpose of staff meetings called at the beginning and end of the year. Although all meetings have some element of ritual or membership-maintaining functions, when that is the main purpose it should not be seen as having some other productive outcome. Understanding of the symbolic or ritual function of meetings is not widespread and programmes of team and staff development might well include ritual awareness as part of the training.

3. **Communications meetings**

Meetings are sometimes justified as a way of transmitting messages and improving communications. They can be occasions when new administrative rules and procedures are announced, key diary dates given, and other minor matters dealt with. The research on communications is unanimous in condemning this as an extremely ineffective method of transmitting messages, and it is certain that if information is given at meetings it will also need to be sent out by another mechanism if it is to register. Top-down communications meetings primarily fulfil a ritual membership-maintaining function for which the transmission of information is an excuse. There is no harm in this so long as key communications are repeated in other ways. The meeting can be used as a place for communication back to managers by staff of attitudes, opinions, uncertainties and unresolved problems. This is clearly valuable and, to make the most of the opportunity, written information relevant to such feedback should be available before the meeting. There is a need for active listening skills by the manager if such feedback meetings are to be successful. Directive or prescriptive behaviour is generally inappropriate.

4. **Advisory meetings**

An advisory meeting is not a place for making decisions. It is a place for collecting ideas and information prior to a decision being made at a later date. The manager may be advising his staff or requesting advice or information. Advisory meetings put a premium on ideas, opinions, judgements and information relevant to a named proposition or problem. From the person seeking advice, the predominant behaviour will be that of listening to what is said and responding to queries. An advisory meeting is appropriate when members accept that while they take part in developing solutions by providing ideas and information, they play no part in making the decision. Confusion over this can be disastrous. It is a source of potential hostility or frustration which can be avoided if there is clarity about the location of the decision-making process.

5. **The collegiate meeting**

The purpose of collegiate meetings is to work through a problem or agenda to an agreed solution or line of action by using the technical skill and knowledge of the membership. The equal status or professional worth of all members is recognised; it is a peer group. Positions are rationally supported, disagreements logically argued, and the conclusion reached is one which all accept in their professional judgement as workable. Tasks groups are included under this heading and in so far as the group may also be responsible for implementing its decisions, as for example in a curriculum revision working party, then it is also an implementation group. For a collegiate meeting to work well, members have to accept that arguments are based on technical criteria and that all relevant information is shared. They also have to be willing to accept and implement a decision once the group reaches concensus. The use of hierarchic power, authority or influence is inappropriate to this kind of meeting and the most common cause of failure is through the inability of some members, particularly in hierarchic positions such as vice principal or head of department, to recognise the essential peer-relationship of the meeting.

6. **Committee meetings**

Members at committee meetings represent various interests and offices in making decisions on matters of mutual interest. Behaviour follows the traditional rules of committee procedures and decisions are normally based on formal voting. Accountability lies not with individuals but with the whole committee and unless members are prepared to accept and implement agreed decisions even when personally opposed to them, a committee approach is inappropriate. In this kind of meeting, tactical and strategic manoeuvring and power plays are accepted modes of participation. Some people, whether as chairpersons or members, develop great skill in influencing the course of events towards a more favourable outcome for the interests they represent. Nevertheless the final agreement is the agreement of all, not of specific members.

7. **The negotiating meeting**

This is not unlike a committee meeting in its general formality but instead of representing a number of interests bound together by mutual concern in the problem at issue, a negotiation contains two or more sides which are only meeting together because they are dependent on each other to arrive at an agreed solution. Each side uses what weapons it has to hand in order to get the best decision for itself. Each side is out to win and make sure the other side loses. Compromises generally have to be made on a quid pro-quo basis. Negotiation meetings require the willingness of members to enter into bargaining procedures. If there is no agreement to bargain the meeting cannot concern negotiations. Each side will have in mind an ideal solution which would give it all it wanted, and a fall-back position beyond which it will not go in any circumstances. The meeting is concerned to find a settlement which falls between these two extremes for both parties. Although tradition has it that it is at the negotiation table that the skills of Machiavelli come to the fore, research evidence suggests this is not so. The most able negotiators turn out not to be men and women of infinite cunning playing their cards very close to their chest, but to be distinguished by their willingness to encourage as open, co-operative and trusting an environment as possible. Good negotiators avoid point-scoring, competitive stances, and all phrases which might act as irritants to the other side. They are skilful listeners and are willing to reveal their inner doubts and feelings about what is going on. They spend time seeking information, summarising arguments, and testing out their understanding of points made by the other side. They particularly avoid getting involved in the defence-attack spirals that are a common aberration of meetings in which there is a clash of interest.

A SUMMARY OF IMPLICATIONS FOR MANAGERS

1. We need to be quite clear about what kind of meetings we wish to hold.
2. We need to ensure that the members of the meeting are clear as to what kind of meeting it is.
3. If the nature of the meeting changes during the course of one session — say from an advisory to a collegiate meeting — we need to signal the change clearly.
4. We should be aware of and counter any ambiguity about where the source of decision-making power lies.
5. As different kinds of meetings require different skills, we need to choose membership for meetings in such a way that the skills of members are matched to the demands of the situation. The chapter on interaction skills outlined the behaviours which members may adopt in meetings. Membership can be compiled to provide the best blend of behaviours. For example, a particular set of meetings might require a high level of initiating, seeking information and summarising. Another set of meetings might require a much higher level of encouraging and co-ordinating.
6. Similarly we will need to match the personality of the staff to the character of the meetings. The person who finds it difficult to drop the trappings of his hierarchic position will not work well in a collegiate meeting. The brainstorming individualist may be unsuited to the formal procedures of the committee.
7. An understanding of the types and functions of meetings will help the manager set up staff training programmes which expand the range and versatility of his staff and improve his own managerial contributions.

Chapter 11

Team development

In much of our day-to-day work as educational managers, we are likely to be involved with groups — governing bodies, academic boards, working parties, project groups, etc. It is a hard fact of modern organisational life that much of our work has to be initiated, monitored and achieved not by individuals working on their own, but working in conjunction with others — both formally and informally.

A characteristic of most teams is that they are usually a fairly small group of people with differing backgrounds, skills and knowledge working together on specific and defined tasks. Members are interdependent in that the successful completion of the task requires contributions from each member. So we can conveniently define our team as being fairly permanent, with members in reasonably frequent interaction, with inter-dependent behaviour aimed at the achievement of some common task.

There is nothing very original in the use of teams. What is relatively new is the application of the team as a conscious and deliberate design structure in organisations, as for example, in the corporate management approach in local government.

THE VALUE OF THE TEAM APPROACH
As an organisational structure, the team possesses strengths and weaknesses. Among strengths we can number the following:

(a) Each member's specialist knowledge and skills can be used and co-ordinated to the achievement of the common task.
(b) Each member has knowledge of the whole work area and individual responsibility for the whole as well as individual parts.
(c) There is a potential of adaptability with a high degree of receptivity to new ideas and new ways of operating.
(d) There is a reduction of functional isolation and parochialism.

Among weaknesses we can include the following:

(a) A lack of clarity in communication and decision-making.
(b) Low economy as a large proportion of the energy of all the members is used in keeping activities going, e.g. the management of relationships of members, explanations and deliberations.

THE OBJECTIVES OF TEAM BUILDING
Many educational managers who have to work with others in a group or team effort express grave doubts about the value of working in that way. They frequently come out of meetings with phrases such as:

'We never seem to get anywhere.'
'It's just a lot of talk, we go round and round in circles.'

'We all seem to be pulling in different directions.'

I want to make a point that is absolutely fundamental to the position argued in this paper. I believe that nearly all of us are unskilful at handling co-operative relationships in groups or teams. The reason for this, I would argue, is that the whole of our educational experience has been competitive. We are judged as better than some, worse than others, with our individual place on the mark list. Our educational experience is also individualistic in that we are judged on our own efforts and we see our work only as something that concerns ourselves and our teacher. What others are doing, and what we do in co-operation with others is of no account.

Being both competitive and individualistic is second nature to us in our work and managing structures and operating methods have been set up with this in mind, so it is not surprising that we are not very happy or effective when we have to work in team. Some of the pervasive habits we demonstrate in team activity are:

Competition:	'I must score all the points.'
Withdrawal:	'This is all a waste of time.'
Lack of trust:	'He will stab me in the back.'
Secretiveness:	'I'm not sharing this with the rest.'
Fight for resources:	'I'm getting my fair share.'
Control:	'I'm going to get my way.'

There is a skill in operating in a team, just as there is in playing golf, wiring up an electronic unit or painting a wall. The key concept in team building is simply the belief that teams of people can be consciously trained within a coherent programme to become more effective.

SKILLS IN TEAM BUILDING

What is involved in skill training in team building? Let us differentiate between two different kinds of skills. When a group of people work together on a complex task, they use their abilities in two ways. One is dealing with the job to be performed in which they use their professional or technical skills. The other is in dealing with other members of the team, the process of human interaction. The interaction between people is a function of the way they think, the way they act, the way they feel, and of the values they respect. It is also related to the environment, how they are affected by it, and what they do to control it.

Task skills are those which are relevant to achieving the task. They are:

1. Defining what the task is.
2. Mobilising the resources and skills needed.
3. Making decisions to achieve the task.

Those skills which are relevant to working with other people are process skills. They are:

1. Understanding the roles played by people in the group.
2. Improving communications between members.
3. Understanding the dynamics of the group.

4. Handling conflict in the group.
5. Increasing co-operative and collaborative activities.

A distinction can be made between **what** is being done and **how** it is being done, i.e. between **task** and **process**. How well we accomplish the task is influenced by what happens in terms of process. Task skills are the necessary conditions for team achievement but are not sufficient by themselves. Sufficiency also depends on process skills. The educational world has traditionally recognised and developed task skills, but it has largely ignored process skills and often discouraged shared effort. It is not surprising that for many adults of today the abilities required to work effectively as a team leader or member of a team do not come naturally.

So team building is a deliberate and planned effort to produce an effective team by the development of the necessary (task-related) and sufficient (process-related) skills.

METHODS OF TEAM BUILDING

One method that has been used by a number of firms in this country is the use of a packaged programme developed at the Massachusetts Institute of Technology by Rubin, Plounick and Fry. It consists of three phases:

Phase I is a diagnostic phase. By in-depth interviewing of all the members of the team and possibly by the use of questionnaires the trainer is able to elicit how the team thinks it is operating and what problems and contradictions have emerged. The information, which often contains direct disagreements as to what the team is supposed to be doing, is fed back to the team. As a result of the subsequent discussion it should be possible to draw up an agenda of the problems that the group now sees.

Phase 2 is concerned with developing skills and awareness. The eight modules, each built round a half-day meeting, aim to develop the ability to clarify objectives and organisational roles and to increase sensitivity and understanding of the team's processes. The kind of areas covered include the following:

Agreement on the goals of the team, on what the team wants to do, on who is doing what.
An understanding of role negotiation, feedback to members of their positive and negative role contributions.
An understanding of the way in which the team proceeds to make decisions; the kind of behaviour manifest by individuals and the team as a whole in working towards performance of the task.
An exploration of how people feel working in the group and the effect feelings have on performance. This might be supported by using encounter techniques or sensitivity training.

Phase 3 is concerned with transferring the skills learned or improved in the previous phase back to the organisation. The team has another look at its objectives and procedures to see if they can now be improved and from that an action plan is drawn up which should be the justification for the claim that this experience in team training has been of benefit.

POSSIBILITIES FOR THE FE COLLEGE

A college can probably not afford this kind of outside consultancy service, and indeed may not desire it, but much can be done within the college if there is a genuine commitment to team training. We suggest the following kinds of team training, all of which alone or in combination have been used in colleges of further education.

Team building by training exercises

One way in which team skills can be developed is to use exercises specifically aimed at diagnosing faults and improving performance in training workshops. The tasks are generally games or simulations and may involve the teams, for example, in building a model or construction of some sort, producing a solution from scattered pieces of evidence, acting in default of complete information, or reaching a concensus on matters which are subjective and value-ridden. Each exercise helps participants work at certain of the team skills. For example one exercise might be to check on the team's capacity to define accurately the task with which it is faced and the way in which decisions were made. Another exercise might examine how far the team made use of all the resources it had available, both personal and physical. A further exercise might explore the capacity of the team to handle conflict and disagreement among its members, or its skill in communicating complex pieces of information.

For whatever purpose the exercise is being used, and many of the standard exercises can be used to achieve a variety of goals, it is essential that the team's performance is observed and feedback on the performance given. This is best done by an experienced facilitator who will find no problems in feeding back critical comment to the group and who will have developed skills of accurate observation and diagnosis. If no such person is available, however, members of the team can act as observers, and that in itself is a powerful educational process both for the observer who has to note carefully what the team is doing and feed back his comments, and for the team which has to cope with critical feedback from one of its own members. There is a strong tendency for observers only to give initially positive feedback and to wrap up any critical comment with so much qualification that the message is lost. A crucial skill needed in all types of team building is the ability and willingness to give strong critical comment on the team or its members in a clear and unapologetic manner. If the team has a reasonable level of trust members will assume feedback comes from a constructive supportive focus and it is unnecessary and counter-productive for the commentator to labour that point. If the team has not reached such a level of trust, the first exercises in team building need to be trust building activities.

This method of team building is particularly valuable at the time when a team is first establishing itself or when it has been operating for some time and is self-confessedly performing badly. It has been used with success by colleges at residential weekends when new departments have been formed from sections taken from several other departments.

Team building by reflection on task performance

A second method of team building is to use the activities of the group in the performance of its expected tasks as the raw material for examination. This has the advantage of operating in a world of reality rather than simulation, and in a purely practical sense it is more easily fitted into the timetable of the members' activity. It does not require residential weekends or other long periods set aside. It does require the team to give time at the end of its session to examine the way in which it has worked at its task and handled the processes involved. It may be convenient to set up a team meeting on a separate day for this reflective diagnosis, but the key characteristic of this method is that the actual work of the team at its tasks is examined regularly by the members of the team. A facilitator is not absolutely essential but very desirable as he will observe processes and behaviour in a way that is impossible for those who are actively taking part in the work. However, part of developing maturity of a team is the capacity of its members to observe what is happening during the task-active sessions and to reflect back on the sessions with a fair degree of recall. It is not solely the responsibility of the facilitator to diagnose and comment: it is primarily a team activity and the facilitator helps focus the team's attention and brings up matters which the team is avoiding or suppressing. An initially attractive method is for the exercise to be video filmed and played back for the whole group to observe and comment. This does away with the need for an observer but it has problems of its own. Handling the observation and feedback becomes in effect another team exercise, and a particularly difficult one at that. It in turn needs critically to be observed and fed back, and so on ad infinitum. The use of video in conjunction with a facilitator or observer from the group may be of considerable help, but if used without them it may create more difficulties than it solves.

Team-building by skills analysis

A third method of team-building is one that is advocated by the Further Education Unit (FEU) in its publication **Teaching Skills**. The basis of this is that in the process of working through the skills which the team needs to accomplish a particular task, the working capacity of the team is itself developed. Such a skills-based approach would at first seem to be unduly limiting, though it is an approach that is commonly adopted by short-term task teams. It would seem to ignore the process skills and some of the tasks skills in its undue emphasis on the definition of the task and the programme to develop the resources for that task. However, much depends on what the required skills are. In the FEU document, the skills required for the successful operation of a team responsible for a vocational preparation-type course (and this would include the programmes in the Youth Training Scheme) encompass the following:

> Student-centred approaches to learning (to include negotiation with student counselling and guidance);
> Curriculum innovation;
> Method innovation (to include use of games, simulations, role play, group work');
> Team co-ordination;
> Team membership;
> Liaison and negotiation;
> Basic skills teaching.

It is clear that these skills include several process skills — counselling, negotiating, working with groups, contributing effectively as a team member, co-ordinating and developing a team. Where this is the case a skills based team training approach can be very effective. The FEU document suggests that if a skills profile is drawn up for each individual, a summation of these can form a team profile which indicates where there is a need for skills development among its membership. It is assumed that not all members need all skills at a high level, but the team as a whole must have sufficient of them.

Example of a team profile

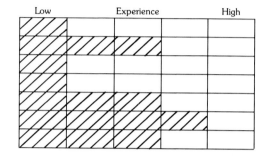

	Low	Experience	High
1. Student centred approach			
2. Curriculum innovation			
3. Method innovation			
4. Team co-ordination			
5. Team membership			
6. Liaison and negotiation			
7. Basic skills teaching			

By aggregating the individual profiles, we see that the team is short of experience in a number of skill areas — student-centred approaches to learning, method innovation, and team co-ordination. Before it is assumed that these are the only areas for attention, however, the team should discuss all seven areas to check that all members have used common definitions and that their experience in, for example, liaison and negotiation is relevant to the tasks which face the team.

The skills-based approach deals well with one aspect of team development — the possession of appropriate individual skills. It also, in the very process of examining individual skills, develops a number of other team skills — openness, risk-taking, trust, communication, co-ordination, decision making — though this may not necessarily be at a very high level. The crucial problem to overcome in this form of team building is to separate out very clearly those functions and activities which are concerned with individual staff development and those which are concerned with improving the operation of the team. There is a tendency to confuse the two, and this is apparent in the FEU document.

Team building by use of questionnaire

The use of questionnaires has considerable advantages. It makes available to the term in a permanent form the assessment by its membership of its salient characteristics. It is a potent diagnostic tool which can help the team take action to develop those behaviours of skills in which it seem deficient. One method of utilising questionnaires is to ask all members of the team of indicate where the team currently is operating and where they would like the team to be in six months or a year's time. When individual responses are summated this will give a clear indication of those areas which, in the view of the team, need attention and those with which the team feels satisfaction. Programmes of team development follow naturally. If, at the end of the period, the questionnaire is again filled in the team can check on its progress and readjust its ambitions for the future.

The use of the Likert Short Management System Questionnaire is illustrated by a team development programme undertaken at North Nottinghamshire College of Further Education for the senior management team. Likert assumes that organisations can be classified on a continuum within which there are four main types:

Type 1 Exploitive — authoritative
Type 2 Benevolent — authoritative
Type 3 Consultative
Type 4 Participative

These are described in Appendix A, pp. 110-111.

The questionnaire reproduced in Appendix B, pp. 111-113, divides its 22 responses into seven areas which are seen as organisational operating practices:

(a) Leadership processes used.
(b) Character of motivational forces.
(c) Character of communicative processes.
(d) Character of interaction — influence processes.
(e) Character of decision-making processes.
(f) Character of goal-setting or ordering processes.
(g) Character of control processes.

Generally there is consistency in responses across all the areas as a style and philosophy of management tend to permeate all aspects of an organisation. In the case of the North Nottinghamshire College, as illustrated in Appendix D, p. 114, the senior management team identified itself as operating in Type 3 consultative system and as aspiring to Type 4 participative system. Within six months, after some conscious team training, the team members were identifying themselves as just within the Type 4 system and had made substantial moves in:

The manner in which motives are used;
The accuracy of upward communication via line level at which formal decisions are made;
The extent to which review and control functions are concentrated;
The extent to which peoples' activities go against or support formal goals.

Another questionnaire which can be used in the same way is McGregor's Team Development Scale, which is reproduced in Appendix C, p. 113.

The value of the questionnaire approach is therefore that:
1. It provides a framework of investiations and analysis by which individual members can think about the activities of their team. This, even on its own, is a useful form of team development.
2. It makes clear those areas in which performance is seen to be unsatisfactory and enables goals to be set for improvement.
3. It indicates the development programme which is appropriate to this particular team and can lead into exercises or task reflection sessions as described above under the first two methods.

THE DEVELOPED TEAM
The purpose of team training is to fashion a developed team. What are the characteristics of such a team? Francis and Young claim that they are as follows:

1. **Effective leadership:** The team manager has the skills and intention to develop a team approach and allocates time to team building. Leadership is shared around the team as appropriate to its needs.
2. **Suitable membership:** Team members are individually qualified and can contribute to the mix of skills and chacteristics that provide an appropriate balance.
3. **Commitment to the team:** Members feel a sense of individual commitment to the aims and purposes of the team, and will devote personal energy to building the team and supporting other members. When working outside the team boundaries they feel a sense of belonging to the team.
4. **Constructive climate:** The team has developed a climate in which people feel relaxed and are able to be honest, open, and take risks within high levels of trust.
5. **Concern to achieve:** The team is clear about what it wants to achieve and works to practicable targets. Energy is mostly channelled into achieving results and checking performance.
6. **Clear corporate role:** The team is clear as to its contribution and importance to the overall organisation.
7. **Effective work methods:** The team has developed systematic, flexible and effective ways to solve problems together.
8. **Well-organised team procedures:** Roles are clearly defined, communication patterns well developed, and administrative procedures support a team approach.
9. **Critique without rancour:** Team and individual shortcomings and errors are examined without personal attack to enable the group to learn from its experience.
10. **Well-developed individuals:** Team members are deliberately developed and the team can cope with strong individual contributions.
11. **Creative strength:** The team has the capacity to create new ideas through the interactions of its members. Innovative risk taking is encouraged and new ideas from members or outside are welcomed.
12. **Positive intergroup relations:** Relationships with other teams have been developed and individuals are encouraged to contact and work with other teams. Joint activities are set up wherever it is beneficial.

From this scheme we can formulate a check list of blockages which a team can use to identify the areas requiring attention:

Is leadership ineffective — apathetic — domineering — exclusive to one person?

Has the team the wrong mix of people? Should some be added? Some taken out?

Are individuals uncommitted, half-hearted in their support, without a sense of belonging?

Is the climate distrustful, suspicious, stressing conformity, suppressing conflict, full of hidden motives and cliques? Is the team not clear what it wants to do, unenthusiastic about doing it, devoting its energy elsewhere?

Is the team unsure where it fits into the organisation, whether it is seen as having any importance, whether any notice is ever taken of it?

Is the team bogged down with poor progress, bad planning, lack of decisions?

Are members unclear about their roles and have conflicting objectives? Do they fail to communicate with each other clearly enough?

Is criticism resented? Is it given to put down the recipient? Is there little learning from past mistakes?

Are members left to work out their own salvation in the group? Are members allowed to be withdrawn or domineering? Are members allowed to stay with nothing more than their professional or technical skills?

Does the team create few ideas? Is it wary of new ideas? Is it worried about risk taking?

Does the team see other teams as competitors? Is it ignorant about other teams?

CONCLUSION

It is for each college or school to decide whether there is a need for teams in its operations. Considerable skills are required for individuals to work together in a team and a team approach to management is not something to be undertaken just for the sake of it. If a team would not do the job better than an individual, then it is certain that the individual will be happier and more effective working on his own. However, for many purposes a team is more appropriate and the rewards to the individual when he is part of an effective team are considerable. These rewards are available through the process of conscious team development.

FURTHER READING

There are few books specifically on team training. The following two books provide the background thinking and some techniques behind the concept of team development and are widely read as general management texts.

LIKERT, R. **New patterns of management.** McGraw Hill, 1961.

McGREGOR, D. **The human side of enterprise.** McGraw Hill, 1960.

Two useful books on team building are:

BERGER, Melvyn L. and P.J. eds. **Group training techniques.** Gower Press, 1972.

Part two of this book contains chapters on building an effective work team, on role negotiations, and on team training experiences at IBM (UK) Ltd.

FRANCIS, Don and YOUNG, Don. **Improving work groups. A practical manual for team building.** La Jala, Calif., University Associates, 1979. ISBN: 0-883-90149-8.

This is an excellent introduction to the process of team building, and contains many suggestions for development exercises.

A major source of exercises is the following series:

PFEIFFER, J.W. and JONES, J.E. eds. **Handbook of structured experiences for human relations training,** Vols. I-VIII. San Diego, Calif., University Associates, issued annually.

APPENDIX A

LIKERT'S DEFINITION OF MANAGEMENT SYSTEMS

System 1
This management system assumes that labour is largely a market commodity, with time freely sold and purchased. It conceives of the manager's job as consisting of decision, direction, and surveillance, relies primarily upon coercion as a motivating force, and makes little or no provision for the effects of human emotion and interdependence. As a result, communication in this system is sluggish, largely downward in direction, and frequently distorted. Goals are established and decisions made by top management only, based upon fragmentary, often inaccurate and inadequate information. This produces disparity between the desires and interest of the members and the goals of the organisation. For these reasons, only high levels of the organisation feel any real responsibility for the attainment of established objectives. This reliance upon coercion as a motivating force leads to an almost total absence of co-operative teamwork and mutual influence and to a quite low true ability of superiors to exercise control in the work situation. Dissatisfaction is prevalent, with subservient attitudes towards superiors. hostility towards peers, and contempt for subordinates. Performance is ususally mediocre, with high costs, excessive absence, and substantial manpower turnover. Quality is maintained only by extensive surveillance and a great deal of rework.

System 2
The management system assumes that labour is a market commodity, but an imperfect one. Once purchased, it is susceptible to periodic emotional and interpersonal 'interferences'. Consequently, to decision, direction, and surveillance it adds a fourth managerial duty: expurgating the annoying effect of subordinate members. This fact permits some small amount of upward and lateral communication, although most is downward, and sizeable distortion usually exists. Policies are established and basic decisions made by upper management, sometimes with opportunity for comment from subordinate supervisory levels. Some minor implementation decisions may be made at lower levels, but only within the carefully prescribed limits set by the top echelon. Managerial personnel, therefore, usually feel responsibility for attaining the assigned objectives, whereas rank and file members usually feel little or none. Very little co-operative teamwork exists, and superiors at lower echelons are able to exercise only moderate true control in the work situation. Attitudes towards superiors are subservient, and hostility is prevalent towards peers, but the absence of open contempt towards subordinates makes dissatisfaction less intense. Performance may be fair to good, although high costs, absence, and manpower turnover frequently occur.

System 3
This management system does not assume labour to be a market commodity. It still reserves to the manager the tasks of decision, and direction, but removes surveillance as a major function. Little recourse to coercion occurs. In their places recognition of the frequently disruptive effects of human emotion is expanded to include employee involvement through consultation. This practice encourages a

110

moderate amount of valid upward communication, although lateral communication is limited by the prevalence of man-to-man, rather than group, decision-making. Communication is, therefore, usually accurate and only occasionally distorted. In line with this, broad policy decisions are made at the top, but specific objectives to implement these policies are entrusted to lower managers for consultative decision-making. For all these reasons, a substantial proportion of the members of the organisation feel responsible for attaining established objectives, and the system makes use of most positive motivational forces, except those which would otherwise arise from group processes. Some dissatisfaction may exist, but normally satisfaction is moderately high, with only some degree of hostility expressed towards peers, some condescension toward subordinates. Performance is ordinarily good; costs, absence, and turnover moderate; and quality problems no cause for major concern.

System 4
This management system assumes that employees are essential parts of an organisational structure which has been built at great cost and necessarily maintained with the same attention and care given more tangible assets. It conceives of decision as a process, rather than a prerogative, with the manager's responsibility consisting, not of himself deciding, but of making sure that the best possible decisions result. In this light, he focusses his efforts upon building an overlapping structure of cohesive, highly motivated, participative groups, co-ordinated by high mutual confidence and trust, communication is adequate, rapid and accurate. Because goals are established and decisions made with the participation of all those affected, objectives are comparatively closely aligned with the needs and interests of all members, and all motivational forces push in the direction of obtaining the established objectives. The closely knit system in addition permits superiors and subordinates alike to exercise great control over the work situation. Employees at all levels are highly satisfied, but without complacency, and feel great reciprocal respect and trust. Performance is very good; costs, absence and turnover are low; and high quality is the natural concern of all.

APPENDIX B
Likert's short management system questionnaire

Organizational Variable				
1. Leadership processes used				
Extent to which superiors have confidence and trust in subordinates	Have no confidence and trust in subordinates	Have condescending confidence and trust, such as master has to servant	Substantial but not complete confidence and trust, still wishes to keep control of decisions	Complete confidence and trust in all matters
Extent to which superiors behave so that sub-ordinates feel free to discuss important things about their jobs with their immediate superior	Subordinates do not feel at all free to discuss things about the job with their superior	Subordinates do not feel very free to discuss things about the job with their superior	Subordinates feel rather free to discuss things about the job with their superior	Subordinates feel completely free to discuss the job with their superior
Extent to which immediate superior in solving job problems generally tries to get subordinates' ideas and opinions and make constructive use of them	Seldom gets ideas and opinions of sub-ordinates in solving job problems	Sometimes gets ideas and opinions of sub-ordinates in solving job problems	Usually gets ideas and opinions and usually tries to make constructive use of them	Always get ideas and opinions and always tries to make constructive use of them

111

Organizational Variable				
2. Character of motivational forces				
Manner in which motives are used	Fear, threats, punishment, and occasional rewards	Rewards and some actual or potential punishment	Rewards, occasional punishment, and some involvement	Economic rewards based on compensation system developed through participation; group participation and involvement in setting goals, improving methods, appraising progress toward goals, etc.
Amount of responsibility felt by each member of organisation for achieving organisation's goals	High levels of management feel responsibility; lower levels feel less; rank and file feel little and often welcome opportunity to behave in ways to defeat organisation's goals	Managerial personnel usually feel responsibility; rank and file usually feel relatively little responsibility for achieving organisation's goals	Substantial proportion of personnel, especially at high levels, feel responsibility and generally behave in ways to achieve the organisation's goals	Personnel at all levels feel real responsibility for organisation's goals and behave in ways to implement them
3. Character of communication process				
Amount of interaction and communication aimed at achieving organisation's objectives	Very little	Little	Quite a bit	Much with both individuals and groups
Direction of information flow	Downward	Mostly downward	Down and up	Down, up, and with peers
Extent to which downward communications are accepted by subordinates	Viewed with great suspicion	May or may not be viewed with suspicion	Often accepted but at times viewed with suspicion; may or may not be openly questioned	Generally accepted, but if not, openly and candidly questioned
Accuracy of upward communication via line	Tends to be inaccurate	Information that boss wants to hear flows; other information is restricted and filtered	Information that boss wants to hear flows; other information may be limited or cautiously given	Accurate
Psychological closeness of superiors to subordinates (i.e. how well does superior know and understand problems faced by subordinates?)	Has no knowledge or understanding of problems of subordinates	Has some knowledge and understanding of problems of subordinates	Knows and understands problems of subordinates quite well	Knows and understands problems of subordinates very well
4. Character of interaction-influenced process				
Amount and character of interaction	Little interaction and always with fear and distrust	Little interaction and usually with some condescention by superiors; fear and caution by subordinates	Moderate interaction, often with fair amount of confidence and trust	Extensive, friendly interaction with high degree of confidence and trust
Amount of cooperative teamwork present	None	Relatively little	A moderate amount	Very substantial amount throughout the organisation
5. Character of decision-making process				
At what level in organisation are decisions formally made?	Bulk of decisions at top of organisation	Policy at top, many decisions within prescribed framework made at lower levels	Broad policy and general decisions at top, more specific decisions at lower levels	Decision-making widely done throughout organisation, although well integrated through linking groups provided by overlapping groups
To what extent are decision makers aware of problems, particularly those at lower levels in the organisation?	Often are unaware or only partially aware	Aware of some, unaware of others	Moderately aware of problems	Generally quite well aware of problems
Extent to which technical and professional knowledge is used in decision-making	Used only if possessed at higher levels	Much of what is available in higher and middle levels is used	Much of what is available in higher, middle, and lower levels is used	Most of what is available anywhere within the organisation is used
To what extent are subordinates involved in decisions related to their work?	Not at all	Never involved in decisions; occasionally consulted	Usually are consulted but ordinarily not involved in the decision making	Are involved fully in all decisions related to their work
Are decisions made at the best level in the organisation so far as the motivational consequences (i.e., does the decision-making process help to create the necessary motivations in those persons who have to carry out the decisions?)	Decision-making contributes little or nothing to the motivation to implement the decision, usually yields adverse motivation	Decision-making contributes relatively little motivation	Some contribution by decision-making to motivation to implement	Substantial contribution by decision-making processes to motivation to implement

Organizational Variable				
6. Character of goal setting or ordering				
Manner in which usually done	Orders issued	Orders issued, opportunity to comment may or may not exist	Goals are set or orders issued after discussion with subordinate(s) of problems and planned action	Except in emergencies, goals are usually established by means of group participation
Are there forces to accept, resist, or reject goals?	Goals are overtly accepted but are covertly resisted strongly	Goals are overtly accepted but often covertly resisted to at least a moderate degree	Goals are overtly accepted but at times with some covert resistance	Goals are fully accepted both overtly and covertly
7. Character of control processes				
Extent to which the review and control functions are concentrated	Highly concentrated in top management	Relatively highly concentrated, with some delegated control to middle and lower levels	Moderate downward delegation of review and control processes; lower as well as higher levels feel responsible	Quite widespread responsibility for review and control, with lower units at times imposing more rigorous reviews and tighter controls than top management
Extent to which people's activities go against or support goals of formal organisation	Such activities exist and do oppose goals of formal organisation	Such activities usually are present and partially oppose goals of formal organisation	Such activities may be present and may either partially support or partially resist goals of formal organisation	Goals and activities are the same: hence all activities support efforts to achieve goals of formal organisation
Extent to which control information (e.g. costs, exam results, reports, etc.) are used for self-guidance or group problem solving by managers and colleagues; or used by superiors in a punishing and policing manner	Used for policing and punishment	Used for policing coupled with rewards and punishments; used somewhat for guidance in accord with orders	Largely used for policing with emphasis usually on reward but with some punishment: used for guidance in accord with orders; some also used for self-guidance	Used for self-guidance and for co-ordinated problem solving and guidance; not used as punishment

APPENDIX C

MacGregor's Team Development Scale

(For each question circle one number between 1-7)

1. **Degree of mutual trust:**

   High suspicion   High trust

   1   2   3   4   5   6   7

2. **Communications:**

   Guarded, cautious   Open, authentic

   1   2   3   4   5   6   7

3. **Degree of mutual support:**

   Every man for himself   Genuine concern for each other

   1   2   3   4   5   6   7

4. **Team objectives:**

   Not understood   Clearly understood

   1   2   3   4   5   6   7

5. **Handling conflicts within team:**

   Through denial, avoidance, suppression or compromise   Acceptance and 'working through' of conflicts

   1   2   3   4   5   6   7

6. **Utilisation of member resources:**

   Competencies used by team   Competencies not used

   1   2   3   4   5   6   7

7. **Control methods:**

   Control is imposed   Control from within

   1   2   3   4   5   6   7

8. **Organisational environment:**

   Restrictive, pressure for conformity   Free, supportive respect for differences

   1   2   3   4   5   6   7

113

North Nottinghamshire College of FE

Comparison of profile of existing organisational characteristics
Senior Staff

		System I	System II	System III	System IV
Leadership	1 2 3				
Motivation	4 * 5 o				
Communication	6 7 8 o 9 * 10				
Interaction- Influence	11 12				
Decision making	13 * 14 o 15 o 16 o 17 o				
Goal setting	18 19 o				
Control	20 * 21 * 22 o				

* P<0.01
0 0.05> P>0.01
- - - - - - - organisation at December 1972
————— organisation at June 1973
—.—.—.— organisation as required at December 1972

114

Chapter 12

Group interaction analysis

Interaction is the basis of all group activity. Whenever people meet together in formal or informal groups, they communicate with each other, and it is this pattern of communicating behaviour that is the subject matter of interaction analysis.

As students of interaction, we will want to know:

What is said;
How it is said;
Who said it to whom;
When it was said;
Where it occurred.

It is not possible to obtain a fine reading of the behaviour in a group on all these areas, but there are methods for partially illuminating and analysing interactive behaviour, which we will describe.

Is this merely an exercise to satisfy our academic curiosity or is interaction analysis useful in a practical way?

It is our belief that people can improve their own skill in interactive behaviour. This increase in skill is helped by training in interaction analysis, because this gives them:

a. Knowledge about their own social behaviour through systematic observation and feedback;
b. Information and concepts which enable them to improve their social performance;
c. An increased ability to analyse, understand and respond to the behaviour of others.

We should emphasise, however, it is only one of a number of methods of improving an individual's skill in social behaviour, and should in any training programme be part of a wider repertoire of techniques.

There are a number of types of information we can observe in groups. In this paper we will consider:

Frequency,
Interaction Flow,
Role Behaviour,
Content Analysis.

FREQUENCY

We can record the total number of contributions made over a period of time by each individual. Clearly it is useful to know that one member, for example, has made more than a third of the contributions and that two others have said nothing at all. The group itself will have to decide whether this is a state of affairs that is

115

desirable, but if some members make few if any contributions then their potential is not being fully exploited, and if one member is making a disproportionately high number, he is likely to be dominating the proceedings. Generally speaking, the more a member talks, the more the rest of the group responds to what he has said.

The number of contributions made does not tell how long a member has been speaking as his contributions can vary from a second to several minutes. Therefore, one can record who it is that is speaking at intervals of five seconds over a period of time. This will distinguish those who speak at length but not very often from those who make short but frequent interventions.

INTERACTION FLOW

We are here concerned with who speaks to whom. It is not very difficult to record, but we have to make the decision as to whether we are using as our measure:

    a. The discrete contributions made by each member,
    b. The time spent in talking by each member.

In the latter case we begin to dintinguish between monosyllabic contributions and lengthy statements, and we normally measure this by recording interaction flow at five or ten second intervals. Whichever method we use we are able to obtain information about the percentage of interaction taken up by each individual and the direction of comment. From this we can find out who is dominating and who is not contributing; or who are high, medium and low contributors, and what is the flow pattern between high, medium and low contributors. We do not know, of course, the content and meaning of the contributions.

The information can be presented either in the form of a matrix or in diagrammatic form, as shown in Diagrams 1 and 2 below and on page 117.

Diagram 1

To

	1	2	3	4	0	Total		% From
1		4	2	6	2	14		28
2	1		1	3	5	10		20
3	2	0		5	0	7		14
4	6	4	5		4	19		38
Total	9	8	8	14	11	50	50	100
% To	18	16	16	28	22		100	

From (appears to the left of rows 1–4)

Interaction flow matrix

There is one further technique, which records the sequence of contributions rather than the flow but does enable us to draw rather similar kinds of conclusions. By simply recording in a linear way the person making each sequential contribution, we can see the patterns of interaction over time. We are able to establish now only how many contributions a person made, but also whether these were scattered throughout the period or mostly at the end or near the beginning. We can also see whether there are trios or duologues establishing themselves. Take, for example, the following sequence:

B F D B H E H B F B A C A C A E H F B F B A C E H D H F H B G H B F G C A C

116

This is the order in which people spoke to a task group of eight. We can see that two sub-groups were present, a trio of members B F H and a pair of members A C. The importance of being able to spot these sub-groups is that by tending to talk among themselves they reduce the extent of interaction they are prepared to have with the whole group. We can also see who are the linkmen (in this case members E and C) who transpose the discussion from one sub-group to another or to the group as a whole. Sub-groups can be transient or stable, and it is, of course, the stable groups that have a significant effect on the work of the group.

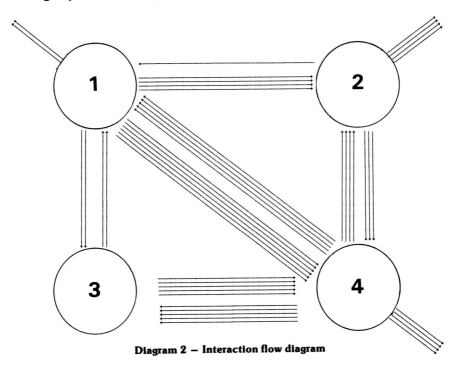

Diagram 2 — Interaction flow diagram

ROLE ANALYSIS

Within each group members take on roles with appropriate behaviours and the way in which the group operates depends very much upon how these various roles combine together over any one period of time. There have been many attempts to categorise these roles so that this can form the basis for detailed observation and analysis of the group's behaviour and operation.

One common categorisation is as follows:

Task roles (i.e. functions required in selecting and carrying out a group task):

1. **Initiating activity:** proposing solutions, suggesting new ideas, new definitions of the problem, new attack on the problem or new organisation of material.
2. **Seeking information:** asking for clarification of suggestions, requesting additional information or facts.

117

3. **Seeking opinions:** looking for an expression of feeling about something from the members, seeking clarification of values, suggestions or ideas.
4. **Giving information:** offering facts or generalisations relating one's own experience to the group's problem to illustrate points.
5. **Giving opinions:** stating an opinion or belief concerning a suggestion, particularly new ideas, new definitions of the problem, new attack on the problem, or new organisation of material.
6. **Elaborating:** clarifying, giving examples or developing meanings, trying to envisage how a proposal might work if adopted.
7. **Co-ordinating:** showing relationships among various ideas or suggestions, putting ideas or suggestions together.
8. **Summarising:** restating suggestions or ideas after discussion, stating group's position at a given point.

Group maintenance roles (functions required in strengthening and maintaining group life and activities):
1. **Encouraging:** being friendly, warm, responsive to others, praising others and their ideas, agreeing with and accepting the contribution of others.
2. **Gate-keeping:** helping all to contribute, keeping the group to its task.
3. **Standard setting:** expressing group standards for use in choosing its content, procedures or decisions.
4. **Expressing group feeling:** summarising what group feeling is sensed to be, describing reactions of group to ideas.

Task and maintenance roles
1. **Evaluating:** measuring accomplishments against goals and standards of group.
2. **Diagnosing:** determining source of difficulties and appropriate next steps. Analysing blocks to progress.
3. **Testing for concensus:** asking for group opinion to see if decision is near, sending up trial balloons.
4. **Mediating:** harmonising, conciliating differences, making compromises.
5. **Relieving tension:** draining off tension through joking or changing context.

Some non-functional roles
1. **Overly aggressive:** working for status by criticising or blaming, showing hostility, deflating others.
2. **Blocking:** interfering with progress, raising irrelevant or tangential issues, rejecting ideas without consideration.
3. **Self-confessing:** expressing personal, irrelevant and non-group points of view.
4. **Competing:** vying with others to produce the best ideas, talking the most, trying to gain leader's favour.
5. **Seeking sympathy:** inducing sympathy for personal problems or misfortunes, self disparaging.
6. **Special pleading:** introducing one's own pet concerns, or philosophies, lobbying.
7. **Horsing around:** clowning, joking, mimicking, disrupting.

8. **Seeking recognition:** calling attention to oneself through excessive or loud talking, extreme ideas or unusual behaviour.

There has been general acceptance that this more or less covers the roles and associated behaviours that are likely to be found in group operations. It is more of a problem however, to find a system of recording the activities of a group that will illuminate the pattern of role behaviour of its members. Content analysis attempts to do this.

CONTENT ANALYSIS

Bales interaction process analysis
This, one of the earlier and still one of the most influential systems, was devised by R. F. Bales in 1950. The hypothesis behind his 12 categories is that contributions of members can be divided into two major areas:

Those related to what he describes as socio-emotional behaviours.
Those related to task-solving behaviours.

Each of these has two contrary aspects. There are negative and positive socio-emotional behaviours, and there are questioning and answering behaviours which are concerned with task-solving. Bales believes that all groups by their nature have to attempt to handle six processes:

Evaluation
Orientation
Control
Decision-making
Integration
Tension management

All his categories are related to these six processes as Chart 1 shows.

CHART 1

Task dimension

Category	Behaviour illustration	Problem area
Answers 1. Gives suggestions	Suggests direction, Solutions. Implying autonomy for others.	Control
2. Gives opinions	Evaluating. Analysing. Expressing wishes or feelings.	Evaluation
3. Gives orientation	Informing. Repeating. Confirming. Clarifying.	Orientation
Questions 4. Asks for orientation	Seeks information or clarification. Seeks confirmation or repetition.	Orientation
5. Asks for opinions	Seeks evaluation, analysis, asks for expression of feelings.	Evaluation
6. Asks for suggestions	Seeks directions, solutions.	Control

Social-emotional dimension

Category	Behaviour illustration	Problem area
Positive		
7. Shows solidarity	Raising others' status, helping, rewarding.	Integration
8. Shows tension — Release	Joking, laughing, showing satisfaction.	Tension-management
9. Agrees	Agreeing, passively accepting, understanding.	Decision
Negative		
10. Disagrees	Disagreeing. Showing passive rejection. Withholding help.	Decision
11. Shows tension	Withdrawing. Seeking help.	Tension-management.
12. Shows antagonism	Deflating others' status. Defending or asserting self.	Integration

The Bales system of recording contributions made by members for subsequent analysis has been widely used, particularly with problem-solving groups. It is, however, a rather complicated system, not easy to use, and has been modified for these reasons into less complex forms. One other problem about it was picked up by Klein, and it is her scheme we now look at.

Klein's interaction schedule

Klein's scheme, which came from her studies of small group interactions and was published in 1961, draws very heavily on the work of Bales. However, she found it necesssary to make a sharp distinction between factual statements and statements that had a value implication — for example:

'One third of those between ages 16 to 19 attend no educational institutions whatsoever.'

This is clearly a factual statement.

'It is quite wrong that only two thirds of this age group attend school or college.'

This is clearly a combination of fact and value which Klein thinks is best described by the word 'view'.

So this gives a schedule as shown in Charts 2 and 3 below and on page 121.

CHART 2

Dimension	Category	Notation
Task related factual	Asks for information Gives information	inf − inf +
Task related combining facts and values	Asks for views Gives views Disagrees Agrees Makes explicit proposals	vi − vi + agr − agr + pro

120

She has a further dimension, expressive of feelings which are irrelevant to the task, two of which are negative and one positive.

CHART 3

Dimension	Category	Notation
Task irrelevant Expressive, evaluative only.	Expresses hostility Expresses withdrawal Expresses friendliness	Expr −h Expr −w Expr +f

The matrix used for scoring contributions also includes a record of who talked to whom. Certainly for team building or organisation development programmes Klein's schedule has proved very useful. One of its weaknesses is the sharp break between task and non-task behaviours, and observers have found it difficult to score behaviours which have both a task and an affective element.

Rackham's behavioural analysis

Rackham and his associates developed this technique originally for social skill training of supervisors within the air transport industry, but have since applied it to a wide range of other occupations and organisations. Rackham has produced a number of sets of behaviour categories and has argued that we should be ready to change and adapt them to meet needs of the specific situation in which interaction is taking place, but the following set is very typical of the general approach. (Chart 4 below)

CHART 4

Category	Description
Proposing	A behaviour which puts forward a new concept, suggestion or course of action (and is actionable)
Building	A behaviour which extends or develops a proposal which has been made by another (and is actionable)
Supporting	A behaviour which involves a conscious or direct declaration of support or agreement with another person or his concepts
Disagreeing	A behaviour which involves a conscious or direct declaration of difference of opinion or criticism of another's concepts
Defending/attacking	A behaviour which attacks another person or defensively strengthens an individual's own position. Attacking behaviour usually involves overt value judgements and often contains emotional overtones
Blocking/ Difficulty stating	A behaviour which places a block or difficulty in the path of a proposal or concept without offering any alternative proposal and without offering a reasoned statement of disagreement. Blocking/difficulty stating behaviour tends therefore to be rather bald, e.g. 'it won't work' or 'we couldn't possibly accept that'.
Open	A behaviour which exposes the individual who makes it to risk a ridicule or loss of status. This behaviour may be considered as the opposite of defending/attacking, including within this category admissions of mistakes or inadequacies providing that these are made in a non-defensive manner.
Testing understanding	A behaviour which seeks to establish whether or not an earlier contribution has been understood.
Summarising	A behaviour which summarises, or restates in compact form, the content of previous discussions or considerations.
Seeking information	A behaviour which seeks facts, opinions or clarification from another individual or individuals.
Giving information	A behaviour which offers facts, opinions or clarification, etc.
Shutting out	A behaviour which excludes, or attempts to exclude, another member.
Bringing in	A direct and positive attempt to involve another.

Rackham invited his readers to feel free to plagiarise his work and many have done so. I developed the list shown in Chart 5, for use at the Further Education Staff College. My first attempt failed to score adequately various kinds of negative behaviour. It proved necessary to revise it by introducing the categories of 'blocking' and 'shutting out'. I originally had a category called 'wandering' which scored various kinds of irrelevancies but it was hardly ever used in the task groups I observed. I make the point to emphasise that categories should be modified and changed as seems appropriate and not treated as sacrosanct.

CHART 5

Behaviour	Description
Directing	Contributions indicating the way a discussion should move. For example, an attempt to move onto another item and close the one under discussion; any attempt to control the programming
Bringing in/ Shutting out	Contributions aimed at bringing someone into the discussion or keeping someone out.
Introducing	Contributions which start off a new line of discussion.
Building	Contributions which develop the topic under discussion, arguing either in favour or against, modifying or expanding. It is sometimes a fine point to decide whether a contribution has diverted the line of discussion enough to be classed as introducing, or whether it is further Building the existing argument.
Blocking	Contributions which put difficulties in the way or attack a person or proposal without giving any reasons. Often expressed in emotional or hostile terms
Questioning	Contributions addressed specifically to one person, to obtain specific information or explanation or comment. It should not be confused with general questions to the group which in fact are statements of a Directing, Building or Introducing nature. Nor should it be confused with a Bringing In contribution, which may be put in the form of a question
Requesting information/ Giving information	No explanation needed
Rounding	Contributions which attempt to summarise what has been said by oneself or others, either accurately or inaccurately
Supporting	Contributions which agree with a previous speaker either briefly or by repeating what has been said at some length
Tension-reducing/ Facilitating	Contributions aimed at clearing the air, breaking tension, facilitating progress particularly when the situation is turbulent, frustrating or intense. Generally done by a humorous remark
Multi-speak	Occasions when more than one member speaks at the same time

An example of using the categories:

Bill:	Well, I think we have thrashed that one around enough. We'll move onto the next point. (DIRECTING)
Deirdre:	But what have we decided, Bill? (QUESTIONING)
Bill:	As I see it, there seems to be a concensus that, while the course is worthwhile, it is not worth the cost and is duplicating other courses elsewhere. (ROUNDING)
Anne:	Yes, that's about it. (SUPPORTING)

Charles:	On the next point of the agenda I want to say straight away that I think this scheme of staff assessment is unethical. (INTRODUCING)
Eric:	Why do you say that? (QUESTIONING)
Frances:	Surely it is obvious. It involves one teacher being subjected to the observation of a group of other teachers and then being told how good or bad he is. That might be putting it crudely but that's what it is really all about (BUILDING)
Deirdre:	Oh no, surely . . .)
Charles:	We can't have . . .)(MULTI-SPEAK)
Eric:	Yes, that's absolutely . . .)
Bill:	Come on, let's have one at a time. (DIRECTING) What were you going to say, Deirdre? (BRINGING IN)
Deirdre:	I don't think Fran has read the paper — it doesn't say that at all. It's supposed to be a self-help group and in any case it's voluntary. (BUILDING)
Charles:	Trust you to support it. (BLOCKING)
Bill (to Charles):	Could you explain exactly what you mean by that. (QUESTIONING)
Deirdre:	I don't think it will be worth listening to. (SHUTTING OUT)
Charles:	Maybe not, but it gets us nearer to coffee time. Sorry, Deirdre. Forget I spoke. (TENSION REDUCING)
Eric:	As a matter of information I have heard from 27 staff who would like to take part. (INFORMATION GIVING)
Bill:	Thanks, Eric. (SUPPORTING). Could I heard from those who have objections to the scheme? (DIRECTING)

Readers might like to analyse the dialogue using Bales' and Klein's schemes.

CONCLUSION. OVERALL ASSESSMENT OF THE GROUP

Whatever system or technique we use for looking at the interactions within a group, we have to interpret the evidence we get against our total impression of the group. In particular we might observe how the group divided its time on various tasks, how it handled overt conflict, how it made its decisions, how it dealt with minority opinions, what kind of group norms were established. There are four conditions, which can become pathological, which the group might exhibit:

The group might show great reluctance to get down to the job in hand. There is always an initial reluctance to do this in the first two or three minutes, but it can be a more prolonged condition. Constant complaints about the room or the chairs, the raising of points of order and long discussions on constitutional points, the challenging of the relevance of the task set or complaints about lack of sufficient information and supporting evidence, may really be devices to avoid facing the group's real problem.

The group might find itself witnessing gladiatorial combat between two or more members who use the meeting to carry on a conflict which exists outside the group and has nothing to do with the job in hand even if that is apparently what they are discussing. Alternatively the group might identify outside enemies and spend time away from the real task in attacking these.

The group can allow itself to become dependent upon one person in the group for doing much of the work. It is likely to do this because it is convenient and allows the work to progress rapidly, but it makes nonsense of the existence of the group.

The group may split up into the kinds of sub-groups we described earlier. Cohesion of the groups is then lost and decisions reached may well be those of part of the group, rather than the group as a whole.

These four conditions in groups are sometimes called:

FLIGHT   FIGHT   DEPENDENCY   PAIRING

Bion, who developed this line of analysis, argues that the group as it moves out of these conditions develops the ability to tolerate ambiguity and ambivalence and to avoid fantasy thinking and splitting. What he means by that is that the members of a mature task group are able to accept and hold conflicting feelings towards a person or institution and avoid the device of splitting them into good or bad categories. Likewise the members move away from illusions that the state of affairs they desire will be brought about 'magically' by some outside agency or person without any work or intervention by themselves.

FINAL STATEMENT

In conclusion, whatever it is that observers or group trainers record and under whatever system, it is essential that there is rapid feedback to members if they are to improve their performance and skill.

The following worksheets which can be used for scoring group interaction are attached as appendices:

Appendix A Bales' interaction process analysis worksheet
Appendix B Klein's interaction process schedule
Appendix C Further Education Staff College Rackham-type worksheet.

APPENDIX A

Interaction process analysis — worksheet

			1	2	3	4	5	6	Total
S.E. +	2.	Shows solidarity: raises others status: gives help: reward							
	2.	Shows tension release: jokes: laughs: shows satisfaction							
	3.	Agrees: shows passive acceptance: understands: concurs: complies							
Task tells	4.	Gives suggestion: direction: implying autonomy for others							
	5.	Gives opinion: evaluation: analysis: expresses feeling/wish							
	6.	Gives orientation: information: repeats: clarifies: confirms							
Task asks	7.	Asks for orientation: information: repetition: confirmation							
	8.	Asks for opinion: evaluation: analysis: expression of feeling							
	9.	Asks for suggestion: direction: possible ways of action							
S.E. −	10.	Disagrees: shows passive rejection: formality: withholds help							
	11.	Shows tension: asks for help: withdraws out of field							
	12.	Shows antagonism: deflates others status: defends or asserts self							

APPENDIX B

Interaction process schedule

From whom?	To whom?	Task related ←− − − − − − − − − − − − −→ expressive										Content reminder
		inf +	inf −	vi +	vi −	(pro)	agr +	agr −	f	h	w	

inf +	gives information	pro	makes explicit proposal	h	expresses hostility
inf −	asks for information	agr +	agrees	w	expresses withdrawal
vi +	gives views	agr	disagrees		
vi −	asks for views	f	expresses friendliness		

Klein, Josephine — **Working with Groups**, Hutchinson, 1966.

APPENDIX C

Worksheet

	Anne	Bill	Christine	David	Erica	Frank	Gail	Henry			Total
Directing											
Bringing in/ shutting out											
Introducing											
Building											
Blocking											
Questioning											
Giving information											
Rounding											
Supporting											
Tension reducing facilitating											
Multi-speak											
Total											

FURTHER READING

A good and short introduction to this topic is the following:

DYAR, D.A. and Giles, W.J. **Improving skills in working with people: interaction analysis.** (Training information paper; 7) Training Services Agency, HMSO, 1974. ISBN: 0-11-360663-X.

Explanations of their particular systems are made by the authors in the following books:

BALES, Robert F. **Interaction process analysis.** Addison-Wesley, 1950.

KLEIN, Josephine. **Working with groups.** Hutchinson, 1966.

RACKHAM, Neil et al, eds. **Developing interactive skills.** Northampton, Wellens Publishing, 1971. ISBN: 0-903084-00-7.

Rackham's book is particularly recommended as a follow-up to Dyar and Giles' text.

BION, W. **Experiences in groups.** Tavistock, 1961.

The diagrams and tables on pp 119 and 121 are adapted from Dyar and Giles' text.

Chapter 13

Some further approaches to interpersonal skills training

In the previous sections of this book I have suggested ways in which people may improve their skills in relating to other people. Many other training methods are currently being marketed to managers and to the general public. This chapter looks at some of these that have particular current popularity, but will make no attempt to cover the whole field. That would require a much longer book.

In looking at these various training methods we can make distinctions based on such criteria as the following:

1. We can distinguish between those that emphasise personal growth as against those that emphasise specific instrumental skills.
2. We can distinguish between those whose main perspective is the organisation and those whose main perspective is the individual.
3. We can distinguish between training programmes that are relatively structured as against those which are relatively unstructured.
4. We can distinguish between those which are mostly controlled by the trainers and those mostly controlled by the members.
5. We can distinguish between those that concentrate on the group and its problems as against those that concentrate on the individual and his problems.

Though training schemes can have any mix of these five characteristics, there is a tendency for there to be at one end of a spectrum, schemes that are unstructured, member-controlled, concerned with the individual and personal growth; and at the other end schemes that are structured, trainer-controlled, concerned with improving skills for the good of the organisation. All the schemes will, however, have elements of each of the opposing qualities. One that is heavily orientated towards improving specific instrumental skills useful to the organisation will also have elements contributing to personal growth. Most unstructured programmes will have some structuring, and the most rigid will have moments of free-flowing uncontrolled activity.

We will not look at the more formal training programmes such as, for example, the Coverdale system. Their purposes and methods are clearly explained in their literature and the prospective client should have no difficulty in understanding what is involved for him and what he is likely to get out of it. The approaches we are concerned with here are those which are generally described as sensitivity training and those which are focussed on individual growth.

The first category of training approaches comprises those in which the group experience is the critical ingredient. In the second category are those training approaches which, while they may use group settings, are primarily concerned with individual growth.

In the first category:	Encounter groups
	T-groups
In the second category:	Gestalt therapy
	Co-counselling
	Body-centred techniques

SENSITIVITY TRAINING

Sensitivitiy training is a method of developing interpersonal skills using various techniques within a context of group experience. The basic characteristic of such training is its experiential nature. By 'experiential' I mean that learning comes from what is actually being experienced by the individual in his/her relationship with other people in the group. The goals of learning are located within the individual. Sensitivity training is not concerned with acquisition of skills and knowledge that lie outside the individual. Its goals are concerned with such areas as:

Developing new insights about oneself as a person;
Analysing one's behaviour and its effects on others;
Understanding better the character of the relationships established with others;
Understanding better one's impact on groups and organisations.

So experiential learning requires a central process dealing with the on-going interaction between that individual and the group. There are common characteristics in all groups involving themselves in sensitivity training.

A concern with the here-and-now

Most learning stems directly from what is occurring at the time or from what has occurred during the history of the group. The most useful data to help a person learn about self and others is that which is immediately and publicly available. Little or no attention is paid to what individuals did before they came into the group. This could mean, for example, that the group does not find out what people's surnames or occupations are.

Feelings as appropriate and valuable material for analysis

In most everyday situations we do not allow ourselves to acknowledge publicly or deal openly with our feelings, whether of warmth or of hostility. We believe that our feelings are not appropriate to reveal in most situations. But constantly devaluing or bottling up our feelings atrophies some essential part of our humanity. Groups create a situation where feelings can legitimately be revealed as material for exploration and analysis.

Self-disclosure

In order to increase self-awareness the individual needs to disclose his feelings and thoughts about himself to others. Jourard described it thus, 'no man can come to know himself except as an outcome of disclosing himself to another person'. It is clearly necessary that the group develops a climate of trust in which self-disclosure and its associated vulnerability is supported rather than exploited by others.

The importance of feedback

This gives the individual the opportunity to find out how his behaviour is seen by others so that he may change it if he wishes. Feedback seems most effective if:

It is given very soon after the relevant behaviour;

It describes specific behaviour rather than general reactions to the whole of the person;

It reveals emotional reactions to another's behaviour without making moral or ethical judgements;

It comes from more than one person.

A climate encouraging an individual to make his own choice about change

In group learning each person undertakes the tasks which seem best suited to him and establishes his own criteria for success or failure. No one else can set tasks for him or lay down changes to be achieved. Much group training takes place in laboratories. The word is used to emphasise the fact that members are encouraged to experiment beyond their usual pattern of interacting with individuals or groups and to learn from such experimentation of behaviour.

GROUP TRAINING

Group training is of various types and uses a range of techniques. Not everyone uses the terms consistently or discretely, but we can distinguish the two major types of groups:

Encounter groups

T-groups (training groups)

Within each there are variants and some of the techniques are common to both. Very often it is no more than a difference in emphasis.

Encounter groups

The primary purpose of an encounter group is that of the personal growth of the individuals who meet to form it. In the words of William Schutz:

'An encounter group has no pre-set agenda. Instead, it uses the feelings and interactions of group members as the focus of attention. The process of achieving personal growth begins with the exploration of feelings within the group, and proceeds to wherever the group members take it. A strong effort is made to create an atmosphere of openness and honesty in communicating with each other. Ordinarily a strong feeling of group solidarity develops and group members are able to use each other very profitably.'

Encounter group is a generic term and there are many variants. Those influenced by Schutz, for example, are likely to follow him in seeing the core of interaction behaviour lying in the individual's efforts to deal with three existential problems. These are:

1. **Inclusion** — feelings of belonging or being separate, of the need to be with people or to be alone;
2. **Control** — feelings of influencing what is happening without invading other people's rights over their lives;

3. **Affection** — feelings of emotional inter-dependence with other people without dependency or counter-reaction.

In Schutz's group it is these three areas that are highlighted, but other groups, such as those influenced by Carl Rogers, have their own particular style. Generally, the effect is similar, even if conceptual schemes are different. There are some common features to encounter groups which tend to distinguish them from T-groups (though some do merge the two):
1. The trainer organises or allows to happen a whole variety of activities other than sitting and talking. These are frequently in the form of physical relating exercises.
2. The trainer involves herself very fully in the group activity, often acting for long spells as a member rather than a trainer.
3. There is an attempt to put the members in touch with their bodies. The assumption is that most people have disassociated their feeling, thoughts and behavioural interactions with other people from their own bodily feelings and reactions so members are encouraged to examine how their bodies feel when they experience anger, rejection, loneliness, excitement.
4. Members are encouraged (though not compelled) to express the way they feel about others in physical as well as verbal terms. Thus feelings of warmth lead to hugging, of competitiveness to wrestling, of rejection to pushing away.
5. Encounter groups are very flexible and borrow any particular technique that seems useful. There is a considerable use of fantasy, of body work and massage, and of Gestalt techniques.

There is a comment of these methods at the end of this chapter.

T-GROUPS
The T-group was first developed at the Tavistock Institute of Human Relationships in the late 1940s by Wilfred Bion. It was an attempt to find a technique of developing leadership and organisation skills for those in employment. It was particularly intended for those working in industrial and commercial firms but was also appropriate to such bodies as churches, colleges and hospitals.

The T-group, as developed by the Tavistock Institute, was concerned with increasing the understanding of the behaviour of small groups. Although this necessarily includes attention to increased self-awareness and awareness of others, the emphasis or focus of concern is on the group as a whole: on the dynamics of group roles, on group norms, on communication distortion, and on the effects of authority on various behaviour patterns.

A T-group is not on-going. It meets for a stated number of sessions and then closes. Typically, this is for a week, but a long weekend or even a series of weekly sessions are common enough. A dozen or so people sit around with no agenda other than that of exploring what happens between them during that time. There is a trainer who takes little overt part and gives no obvious direction. The trainer's purpose is to facilitate or comment on the processes taking place without obtruding or getting in the way. To an outsider the trainer would appear to do very little except sit and watch. The members do nothing much except talk or keep quiet. Although much non-verbal communication takes place, members do not normally more around or relate physically.

Over the past few years, a variant of the Tavistock Group has developed from the Massachussetts Institute of Technology National Training Laboratory (NTL). This method places much more emphasis on personal growth and the individual within the group, and rather less on group processes. Trainers become more heavily involved, and do not sit back as observer/consultants in Olympian detachment from the group.

The NTL type of group now finds more favour in this country than the Tavistock group. The major umbrella organisation concerned with group training of all types, the Group Relations Training Association (GRTA), tends to prefer the NTL model. However, it is only a difference of style and emphasis, and many trainers work at different times with both styles of group.

GROUP PROCESSES

Both T-groups and encounter groups are sufficiently similar to consider together from this point on. Various writers have developed frameworks to describe what habitually occurs in the history of a group. The one we examine here is that of Bennis and Shepard. They see two major obstacles inhibiting the growth of the group. The first concerns authority or influence in the group. Since trainers, against expectations, refuse to lead the group, who will? The second concerns the degree of closeness or warmth members wish to experience, the freedom they want in the group to share and deal with affective feelings. So for Bennis and Shepard, questions of power and intimacy are at the root of social relations within the group.

They see people operating as dependent, counter-dependent or independent — though most individuals have all these characteristics to an extent. Dependents are defined as people who prefer clear tasks, preset rules and an acknowledged leader. Counter-dependents dislike rules, distrust authority leaders and prefer free-wheeling situations. Independents tend not to find power a big issue in their lives. They deal calmly with leadership issues when they become important, feeling neither dependent on nor aggressive towards rules and authority figures.

Bennis and Shepard also see people operating as over-personals, counter-personals and personals. Over-personals are defined as those who want to become as intimate and loving as possible, counter-personals as those who resist or even flee from sharing their feelings with others, and personals as those who can handle matters of intimacy and warmth without too much conflict and with a degree of calmness and rationality.

In the life of a group, power issues typically dominate its first phase. Within this there are normally three sub-phases. The first is characterised by dependence. Members are looking for the leader, for the rules, for a structure, and there is some disorientation at the failure of these to become apparent at once. In the second sub-phase there tends to be a battle between dependents who start to organise a set of rules and authority roles, and counter-dependents who reject this. There is a tendency to break into sub-groups and the issue of leadership becomes critical. Often the trainer or a surrogate is heavily attacked. In the third sub-phase, the conflict should be resolved. Mostly through the work of independents, the group develops its own internal authority system and is able to dispense with any dependency on the trainer. Occasionally the trainer is asked to leave.

In the second phase of the group's activity, questions of intimacy begin to dominate. At first the group is in a state of euphoria. It has been through a rough time and has triumphed. Most people feel good with each other and happy in the group. Some want to stay in this phase because it is so comfortable, but the group eventually moves into issues about the accepted depth of interpersonal contact. Here the battle wages between over-personals and counter-personals. Sub-groups again form and engage with each other, but the membership is different from the earlier phase. The final sub-phase occurs when the personals manage to reconcile the opposing attitudes and reach a consensual position. They are helped by the fact that the group becomes aware that it is reaching the end of its time. Various closure activities and behaviours become apparent. The very last session is generally very warm and good, with feelings freely expressed of experience of intimacy and authenticity in relationships with others.

Of course, Bennis and Shepard recognise that the actual course of a group is chaotic and does not follow exactly this ideal model. But underlying the confusion and ebbing and flowing, many trainers have found the two themes of power and intimacy developing more or less in the way described.

THE EFFECTS OF SENSITIVITY TRAINING

Adverse effects

There is a great deal of bizarre myth or fantasy as to what happens in T-groups, encounter groups or similar kinds of human relations training. One writer described a T-group as 'a psychological nudist colony in which people are stripped bare to their attitudes'. There is a common belief that members are put under great pressure which results in dramatic cases of breakdown, and many others retire having suffered various kinds of psychological damage. In fact, the average group consists of pretty normal people doing normal things under the eye of a normal trainer.

It is, however, true that some cases of psychological damage have been recorded, and it is proper that this area has attracted much research. Although research into this kind of group training is notoriously difficult to set up and interpret, there seems general agreement that psychological damage is a minimal risk and that where it occurs the condition already existed ready to break out and the group experience merely provided the arena in which it could do so.

Positive effects

What is sensitivity training aiming to do? Dunnette and Campbell list the following. To:

1. Increase a person's insight and awareness about behaviour in social contexts by learning how others perceive and interpret behaviour as well as gaining knowledge of why and how a person behaves in different social situations;

2. Increase sensitivity to the behaviour of others by becoming aware of the full range of verbal and non-verbal stimuli as well as by developing the ability to infer correctly how others are feeling or reacting;

3. Increase awareness and understanding of processes that facilitate or inhibit the functioning of groups;

4. Sharpen diagnostic skills relevant in social and inter-personal contexts;

5. Augment behavioural skills so that an individual can intervene more successfully in social and inter-personal contexts;

6. Induce a pre-disposition to analyse interpersonal relations so as to achieve more productive and satisfying outcomes.

Before we look at the results of research on the effects of sensitivity training, it is worth making two points. Firstly, no one has the same learning needs and, whereas one member may learn a great deal because he needs to, another may learn much less because he has not that degree of need, but both learning experiences are equally valuable. Training is designed so that multifarious learning needs can be satisfied at various levels and for the amount of learning to be under the control of the learner. Secondly, not everyone needs or wants to change but most people need to test out certain critical questions about themselves. Having found some answers, they may as likely be confirmed in their current position as encouraged to change.

Accepting these two points, there are seven areas where research suggests group training might have effect. The evidence is that:

1. Learning or change does occur in a significant number of people undergoing training, and it is of the kind intended;

2. T-group and similar forms of training are very potent vehicles for learning, as compared with alternative forms of learning;

3. Listening skills improve substantially;

4. There is an increase in interpersonal perception, that is, the skill in seeing others as they are and/or perceive themselves to be;

5. Members change their perception of reality after training. In particular, they see work as more human and less impersonal, clear connections between satisfying interpersonal needs and work effectiveness, personal needs as a more significant part of work problems, less need to lay responsibility on others for work problems;

6. Members learn to perceive better the difference between their actual self and their ideal self. (This is how I am — this is how I would like to think I am);

7. Though on the basis of little research, the self-esteem and self acceptance of members increases. This is indeed a fundamental meta-goal of the advocates of T-groups and encounter groups. Underlying the notion of any individual's inter-personal competence is that:

   He has confidence in self as well as regarding self highly:
   His experience of self is confirmed by others;
   He feels he is able to express his central needs as well as to utilise his central activities;
   He can, to a satisfactory degree, set his own goals and feel psychological success in attaining them.

These seven findings must be regarded as provisional. Probably 95% of all human relations workshops go unstudied and the research into the remaining 5%

is bedevilled with difficulties. Nevertheless, the findings seem to match up with the commonsense or subjective views of trainers and would be the expected outcomes, given the nature of the learning experience provided.

THE TRANSFER OF LEARNING
A commonly expressed concern about sensitivity training is that although it may have a profound and beneficial effect on the individual during training, he has great problems in readjusting to the 'real' world on his return and, indeed, may come back less able to work well in his organisation than before. Clearly, if this were a common result, employers would not invest on such a scale as they do in sending their employees on this kind of training. Nevertheless, the transfer of learning is a real problem, and undoubtedly individuals do have difficulties in returning to work with new insights, understandings about themselves and others, styles of relating that are more honest and open than before. In the words of one writer:

> 'How can one transfer the climate of trust, of emotional support and acceptance for what one is from a T-group into a wider organisation that more frequently than not shares different values, different norms, and expectations?'

Sheldon Davis puts some of the common issues when he writes:

> 'Say a man has a good experience. He comes back to the job full of new values — and sits down in the same crummy atmosphere he left a week before. He may be changed, but his environment isn't. How can he practise confrontation with a boss and secretary and colleagues who don't even know what it's all about? In a few weeks he's either completely dazed or has reverted in self-defence to the old way.'

Furthermore, it is possible that the way in which customary authority systems are deliberately destroyed in the T-group may leave participants very uncertain how to react to, or exercise, authority when they return to their organisation. Most of the experience at a laboratory workshop are not, on the face of it, related to the situation back home. The relevance to work conditions of much of the material discussed in T-groups is not obvious or direct.

A final difficulty is that there is not the continuous reinforcement that is necessary when individual learning is transferred into an organisational context. If substantial reinforcement is not provided, many individuals may feel frustrated at work and relapse to re-learning the habits and norms of the existing system.

To point up these difficulties is not, however, to deny the value of sensitivity training. There are costs and these can be minimised or increased according to the way the training and re-entry is handled. Problems are minimised when groups in training are complete groups taken from their place of work, and when the issues dealt with are related back to conditions in the home organisation.

PERSONAL GROWTH TRAINING
We now look at three approaches to training which concentrate on the individual and his personal growth. Lowen defined happiness as 'the consciousness of growth', and much recent activity in training and psycho-therapy has been based

134

on the metaphor of growth. It implies firstly that the process of growth is natural, secondly that for most of us there are blocks and impediments to our growth that are causing us to become stunted or twisted, and that the purpose of training is to remove these. If we ask — 'growth towards what?' we are likely to come up with generalised statements such as:

increased capacity for love;
greater energy and excitement in life;
celebration of our abilities;
greater creativity and pleasure;
acknowledgement of the legitimacy of our feelings and emotions

Such statements may seem unsatisfactory and vague, but if we express it in terms of what growth is not, it has a harder edge of meaning. Growth rids us of:

unnecessary restriction to our experience of life;
anxieties, fears and angers derived from concern about how other people view us;
archaic feelings from bad periods of our childhood;
repetitive patterns of behaviour and rules of conduct that have ceased to have any relevance.

There are many growth technique programmes and systems, some of them bordering on the apparently bizarre (although none should be prejudged). Three are particularly important not only because they are very popular, but because they have been having a general influence on many other kinds of training.

GESTALT THERAPY

Gestalt therapy was developed by Fritz Peris from the gestalt psychology of Kohler and Koffa. It has become a common element in management training programmes. Even when not designated by name, it often informs other approaches. Of all the systems described in this book it is the one which is most difficult to convey in words and which really needs to be experienced in order to make an individual evaluation of its benefits. Its major principles are as follows.

Principles of gestalt therapy

1. We experience life as patterns (gestalten) of activity and perception. We have a primary drive to complete or close the pattern and thus achieve satisfaction, and our various problems are caused in part by incomplete activities which we carry around with us. We all have our 'unfinished business', maybe buried deep or maybe very much in our consciousness, and until we deal with it and complete the gestalt, it will cause us difficulties and take up energy we cannot afford. For example, we might have had a row with a colleague which we know we have eventually to sort out, and until we do, it will one way or another get in the way of our other business.

2. The concept of the complete pattern extends to the individual human organism. The body, the mind and all our associated feelings, perceptions emotions and thought form one pattern. We have a tendency to break this pattern into discrete parts, to split ourselves, so that our body and mind become separate entities. We get out of touch with the messages given to us

by our body because of the primacy we give to the thinking process of the mind. One of the purposes of Gestalt therapy is to get the two working harmoniously together, with equal attention given to the messages of each.

3. The individual is a part of his environment and cannot be understood apart from it. Gestalt therapy looks at the way people interrupt their contact with the environment and thus prevent themselves satisfying the needs they have at that moment. Such interruptions come through learned patterns of behaviour which may have made sense when we first acquired them as young children but now simply get in the way of our experience of the environment. There are five ways we can pervert or distance ourselves from our environmental contact.

(i) **Introjection.** This occurs when a person deals with the world through the application of undigested rules, prohibitions, injunctions, and attitudes, thus limiting the choices of behaviour open. 'We have always done it this way.' 'Grown women don't do that.'

(ii) **Projection.** This occurs when we identify in other people qualities we are carrying around ourselves. For example, a person very worried about his own competence may spend much time labelling others as incompetent.

(iii) **Confluence.** This occurs through a person's inability to perceive a boundary between self and the environment. This is the situation of the new-born infant, and can in a limited form survive in adult life. Confluence leads to excessive identification with the organisation or the family or a loved person.

(iv) **Retroflection.** In this case the feelings a person has towards people, objects or events outside himself are redirected back on himself. So a person who feels angry towards his boss may not be able to express this and deals with the emotional energy he has by turning the anger inward and feeling guilty or inadequate.

(v) **Egotism.** This occurs when a person steps outside himself and takes on the role of commentator on what is going on between self and environment. The person who thinks dispassionately and analyses the feelings between himself and his boss rather than expressing them or taking some kind of appropriate action is in a state of egotism.

In each of these five cases there has been a break in the normal way of experiencing the environment:

Introjection — the person takes over part of the environment;
Projection — the environment is host for what originates in self;
Confluence — the boundary between self and environment disappears;
Retroflection — the boundary bounces back feelings that belong outside;
Egotism — there is a gap created between self and environment.

4. The point of gestalt therapy is to help the person experience and be aware of the world around him moment by moment. Much of our time is spent thinking of the past or the future. We worry about what we did, we rehearse

what we are going to do, and we allow the past and future to invade the present to such an extent that we are prevented from fully experiencing the world we are in. It is a common happening for a person to sit through a meeting with someone else and not notice the room or furniture, the clothes of the other person, the sounds outside the window, the smell, let alone some key messages from the other person. We wasted that moment of living by dwelling on the past or future. The rediscovery of immediate awareness is a prime purpose of gestalt training.

Ground rules of gestalt therapy training

Gestalt therapy in practice is more a general orientation around which numerous variations are freely developed than a set of specific techniques. It does, however, have very clear ground rules which arise directly from its general principles.

1. In gestalt workshops members can only deal with the 'here and now', what is happening to them in the group at that moment. If they start bringing in problems and feelings from the past, they are likely to be asked — 'how are you feeling about it now?' or 'What is happening to you as you think about it?'

2. Each person has to take responsibility for all his statements and therefore uses the pronoun 'I' rather than 'you', 'we', 'one', 'people' etc. 'No one likes . . .' is replaced by 'I don't like . . .', 'Everyone knows . . .' by 'I think . . .'.

3. Questions beginning with 'why' are not used because they enable an individual to deal with the question in his head and think up various responses which end up with him 'talking about' instead of experiencing and learning. Thus, 'why are you so abrupt in meetings?' can invite any number of plausible explanations which do not help the person get any new under-standing about his behaviour. Furthermore 'why' questions are often a disguised form of statements by the questioner which needs to come out in the open. A more useful statement would be, 'I find your abrupt manner in meetings disturbing to me.'

4. Gestalt workshops try to discourage members from being clever academics. Experiences are described in the simplest possible manner. Over-elaboration is avoided as something that begins to destroy the immediacy and reality of the experience. Interpretations are even more avoided as a distortion and distancing away from contact with the environment.

These ground rules have spread beyond gestalt workshops and are incorporated very generally into training workshops of all kinds.

GESTALT THERAPY TECHNIQUES

Although gestalt workshops are extremely adaptable and flexible, using whatever techniques seem to open people up to a wider repetoire of experience and response, there are a number of very characteristic gestalt techniques.

Awareness training

This has three particular aspects. Firstly it concerns awareness of what is around in the environment minute by minute, and aims to increase an individual's capacity to see, hear, touch, smell and taste. Various exercises are used to recapture this capacity which is highly-developed in the child but is often much diminished in adulthood, partly by a preoccupation with the past and future rather than experiencing the present moment, and partly by repetitive patterns of behaviour. Adults tend to restrict their activities to established patterns. They always walk the same way home, follow the same routines and take part in the same rituals and pastimes. Gestalt training encourages individuals to experience some of the things they have put behind them — often quite simple things like walking a different way home, climbing a tree, lying down on the grass and smelling the earth.

Secondly awareness is developed by what is happening to the body minute by minute. The individual is encouraged to listen to his body. He pays attention to the following: irregularities in breathing, swallowing, clearing the throat, coughing, muscle-tightening in the jaw, hand, foot, back and neck, facial signs such as furrowing of the brows, smiling and frowning, signs of agitation such as foot and finger tapping, unnatural rigidity or passivity of the body, holding parts of the body, stroking parts of the body, blinking, closing and shifting of the eyes. Various exercises are used to bring the individual into awareness of what is happening in his body and help him explore the meaning of this for him.

Thirdly individuals develop awareness of their emotions as they experience them minute by minute. These three together — the experience of the outside world, the physical sensations of the body and the feeling of emotions — constitute the continuum of awareness.

Two-chair work

This technique involves the individual exploring the splits within himself by taking the part alternately of two conflicting elements and engaging in a dialogue. For example, someone who has a strong moral code and also yearnings for a free and easy life would alternatively take each side and create a dynamic dialogue. It works particularly effectively for cases of projection, introjection and retroflection. It is a very powerful and searching technique which often leads to new insights and consequent adaptations of behaviour, but it needs the supervision of a skilled trainer. Examples of the two-chair technique in operation are given in Fritz Perls' book, **Gestalt Therapy Verbatim.**

Dreams, fantasies, imagery, drama and art

Gestalt therapy makes much use of dreams and guided fantasies as a way of getting in touch with a persons unfinished business. The therapist has to be intuitive, creative and imaginative in looking for the particular approach that will work best. There are examples of Perl's work in **Gestalt Therapy Verbatim.** Careful attention is paid to the imagery a person uses. In a more structured manner, individuals are encouraged to take part in spontaneous drama or draw images which reflect aspects of their life view and these form the basis for subsequent exploration.

It is important to emphasise that gestalt therapy is a very open approach which uses whatever technique is likely to bring the individual more into awareness of his environment, his emotions, or his body sensations. 'It is an orientation to experience which is dynamic and flexible in which the individual is open to all possibilities' (Clark and Fraser).

CRITICISMS OF GESTALT THERAPY

The results of gestalt training, if successful, should be that the trainee is more aware of what is happening inside him and in his relations with other people and has a greater ability to deal with what is, rather than what might be or should be. He will have more choices open to him, a more flexible and creative approach to the people around him, and a greater concern to find ways of living a satisfying life.

Critics of gestalt therapy training generally agree that at the worst it is likely to do very little harm. They accept the important contribution it has made in emphasising the continuum of awareness and in pattern completion, but argue that it goes too far in its suspicion of verbal analysis and interpretation and of the individual's remembered past experiences.

BODY-RELATED SYSTEMS

There are a number of training processes that have become increasingly prevalent in management training programmes in the past few years which involve body work of one kind or another. There are numerous body-balancing, body integration and massage systems, but three in particular stand out: the bioenergetic school particularly associated with Lowen, Ida Rolf's technique known as 'rolfing', and the Alexander system of Moshe Feldenkrais.

At the heart of them is the very simple belief, accepted as commonplace in Greek and Roman civilisation, that the body, mind and soul are an integrated whole. The health of one is the health of the others, damage to one is damage to all three. This holistic view was abandoned by the Christian Church which, at various times in its history, was suspicious both of the mind and the body. Its modern revival dates from the work of Wilhelm Reich, the maverick colleague of Freud. Reich's great contribution was to affirm the central role of the body in any theory of personality or practice of psychotherapy. He was concerned with the chronic muscular tensions nearly all people have in their body, and he referred to the total pattern of such tensions as 'armouring'. He so described them because he believed their function was to protect the individual from painful and threatening emotional experiences. Reich hoped that by working on these body blocks, he could eliminate a person's anxieties and neuroses and enable him to live a happy and creative life with the body in harmony with the mind. Reich was somewhat obsessional in his approach, and it was left to his pupil Lowen to develop his ideas into the much richer and more complex system of bioenergetics. Lowen thought it naive to expect deeply structured problems of personality to be easily resolved by body manipulation techniques.

The bioenergetic approach starts from the assumption that most of us have misused our bodies for years, and we now have chronic deep-seated muscular tensions which lead to unnatural bodily functioning — unnatural in the sense that we do such basic things as breathing and standing in ways that the body was not designed to do, and which it finds difficult to cope with. This arises from our concern to surpress feelings of fear, anxiety, pain and anger. We erect psychic defences of denial, distrust, rationalisation and projection; a necessary mechanism in this process is the channeling of energy into body armouring. The defences erected to surpress the feeling of anxiety are expressed in physical muscular tensions.

It follows that changes in personality are conditional on changes in bodily function, for example on deeper breathing and increased motility. Working on the body blocks enables us to change our psychic defences for authentic encounter with other people and the environment, and releases supressed feelings which have perverted not only our interactions with other people but also out body itself. Should any of this seem fanciful, consider how many people manage to breathe with hardly any use of the diaphragm. One of the effects of constant anxiety is to put a muscular block on the diaphragm; part of the treatment of anxiety is to release this muscular block and practise deep and natural breathing.

Part of the argument for bioenergetics is that contemporary life has accelerated the process of divorce from the body. The culture we live in is not geared to the values and rhythms of the living body but to those of machines and material productivity. Alienation is not just the estrangement of man from nature and his fellow man, but also the estrangement of the person from his body. This has led to a denial of pleasure, creative activity and all that life has to offer in favour of worry, guilt, anxiety, and a concern for power, prestige and possessions. Bioenergetics aims to redress the balance. In Lowen's words, 'Most people go through life on a limited budget of energy and feeling. Bioenergetics is the study of human personality in terms of the energetic processes of the body. It aims to help a person open up his heart to life and love.'

The close connection between the quality of our interaction with other people and the characteristics of our bodily abuse is the basis for the various programmes of change offered by bioenergetics, by rolfing (which concentrates on structural integration through vertical alignment) and other similar systems. The programmes are intended to improve our interpersonal relations by improving the way we use our body — by breathing deeply, standing or sitting with proper balance, relaxing the muscular tensions in our neck, shoulders and stomach. Each person will have to test out the validity of this claim for themselves. Many participants have claimed great benefit from the programmes in increasing their interpersonal and managerial effectiveness, and at the least a person newly considering these approaches should suspend his prejudices (though not his common sense) and give them a fair trial.

CO-COUNSELLING

Those trained in co-counselling work in pairs and normally meet in their own homes. Training in co-counselling skills is a short though intensive process, lasting the equivalent of about four or five days, and on completion co-counsellors become part of a network. The idea of the network is that any member can arrange a co-counselling session with another member whenever he feels the need. The network is a co-operative resource and the contract of belonging to it is that the member is available to any other member. In practice it is very common for two members to meet on a regular basis, say once a week, and very seldom get involved with others in the network, but the total resource is there for those who need it.

Co-counselling is predicated on a number of critical assumptions about the nature of the counselling relationship.

Firstly the two people involved in a session are assumed to be in an absolutely equal relationship. In a traditional counselling session, one person is the counsellor with skills, perceptions and insights, and the other is the client who has needs which the counsellor can satisfy. However skilful the counsellor, this is bound to be a dependency relationship and its usefulness to both parties is limited by that fact. In co-counselling the two members take it in turn to be client and counsellor. Sessions normally last one hour each way, but however long they last, both must have exactly the same amount of time. This is a very strict rule and reinforces the fact that neither is more of a client or more of a counsellor than the other.

The second assumption is that the client is in charge of his session. He decides what contract he wants with the counsellor; he makes decisions whether to accept the interventions or suggestions of the counsellor and it therefore follows that he is responsible for the success of the session, not the counsellor. This takes an enormous burden off the counsellor who, in the traditional set-up, is likely to be continually assessing his own skill in performance and feeling guilt or inadequacy if the session does not seem to be going well. Co-counselling stresses client skills as against counsellor skills. The client, if he is to take responsibility for his time and decide how to use it, needs to develop the appropriate skills. This is why co-counselling training is as much about training the client as the counsellor, and in that it is a fundamental departure from all other forms of counselling. The client can ask for nothing more than one hour of full attention. She may wish for nothing more than active listening while she herself uses her skills to work through her problems. Alternatively, she can give the counsellor permission to offer suggestions and facilitations but with no guarantee that she will accept them. The client can either work on whatever is uppermost in her mind or search deeper for temporarily submerged material.

The theory behind co-counselling, as distinct from the myriad ways people actually use it in practice, is that we are all using a great deal of energy to surpress events which are associated with feelings of anger, pain or grief. Co-counselling skills offer the individual an opportunity to allow these feelings to come to the surface and express themselves in a moment of catharsis. This has two effects. It normally completes the business and it does not trouble us any more. For example if we have long held resentment about a particular teacher who taught us at school, or unexpressed grief at the loss of a friend, after the expression of the feeling we can see the incident as finished. Secondly the energy which we have used to keep the feelings supressed is now released for more productive use.

The client learns the skills of exploring areas where feelings are locked and energy is being wastefully used; similar skills are used by the counsellor when he makes suggestions to the client. The skills are not difficult, but they do need to be acquired in a workshop run by a qualified co-counsellor trainer.

The client does not have to search for submerged matter, nor does he have to work through to catharsis. The whole point of co-counselling is that the client is in charge and can decide how to use the session. He may simply wish to explore a work problem, looking at the various options open to him, examining his feelings in relation to each, testing out or rehearsing possible behaviours. The advantage of co-counselling is that those participating have an hour of someone else's time on no other terms than the ones they themselves set up. The only condition is that they offer the same amount of time to the person who has listened to them. For the manager beset with problems and who, like everyone else has his own personal anxieties and lives with the pressure of his past history, co-counselling offers an attractive framework at a number of levels — problem-resolution, stress-reduction, energy-raising, freeing feelings, dealing with the events locked deep within us, and for celebrating good feelings and successful accomplishments.

Co-counselling developed in the USA as 're-evaluation co-counselling' under the leadership of Harvey Jackins. A less authoritarian alternative has developed in Europe where John Heron has been the major influence. Several networks exist in Britain. Training courses are provided by the Human Potential Research Project at Surrey University.

BRIEF NOTES ON SOME TRAINING APPROACHES NOT CONSIDERED IN THIS BOOK

Meditation techniques. These are not confined to hippies and monks in saffron robes. Meditation is now widely used in management training in industry and commerce, mostly as a method of coping with stress. It is not necessarily a passive technique. Dynamic meditation, in contrast to transcendental meditation, is fairly active and involves considerably more than sitting cross-legged in contemplation.

Some courses concentrate on exploration of the regions beyond ordinary awareness the spiritual, mystical and transcendental elements of our experience which are concerned with the relationship of the individual to the universal. One well-established body concerned with such areas is the Psychosynthesis and Education Trust, but wide variety of courses are on offer ranging from those deriving from oriental wisdom to those concerned with astrological or cosmic influences.

Neuro-Linguistic Programming (NLP). This system is rapidly rising in popularity. It is based on the work of Milton Erikson and is made available in the books of Richard Bandler and John Grinder. It has much to say about behaviour in counselling or one-to-one sessions.

Behaviour Modification. Its techniques are based on the learning theory of behavioural psychologists such as Skinner. It concentrates on the use of positive reinforcers to develop desired behaviour and extinguish undesired behaviour.

Stress Workshops. Most of the systems discussed in this book have as part of their effect a greater capacity to deal with stress, but such is the current concern with the adverse effects of stress at work that many workshops devoted solely to managing and reducing stress are now available. Some techniques, such as bio-feedback, have been developed specifically for stress reduction.

CONCLUSION

Value statements underlie most of the work done in sensitivity training; these should be stated as such rather than as self-evident truths. The over-riding value statement is that we should attempt to develop a more humanistic approach to how people can relate at work and in other social settings. Such an approach is taken to include:

1. A belief in the value of expanding people's consciousness and self-awareness, in particular, so that they become aware of the choices that are available to them.

2. A belief that investigation and exploration of the human condition is legitimate and necessary and that the very process of enquiry is itself liberating.

3. A belief in the value of authenticity in interpersonal relationships, that is, the ability to express openly and fully what one is experiencing at the feeling and thinking levels in such a way as to encourage the other to do likewise.

4. A belief in the value of co-operative concepts of authority relationships rather than of power or coercive concepts.

It is unlikely that people who do not accept these as important or even proper values will accept the validity of sensitivity training. For those who do undertake such training, there is the hope that it will lead to more productive and creative ways of living and working together.

FURTHER READING

There are two accounts of psychotherapy which refer to the major schools and systems.

KOVEL, J. **Complete guide to therapy: from psychoanalysis to behaviour modification**. Harmondsworth, Penguin, 1978. ISBN 0-14-021981-1.

BROWN, Dennis and Pedder, Jonathan. **Introduction to psychotherapy** Tavistock, 1979. ISBN 0-422-76680-1.

On T-groups and laboratory training, a very good introduction with full references is:

BLUMBERG, Arthur and Golembiewski, Robert. **Learning and change in groups**. Harmondsworth, Penguin, 1976. ISBN 0-14-080574-5.

There is an excellent short introduction to gestalt in:

CLARK, Neil and Fraser, Tony. **The Gestalt approach: an introduction for managers and trainers**. Roffey Park Management College, 1982. ISBN 0-907-41601-2.

A more thorough exploration of gestalt therapy with a strong theoretical section and a series of experiments for developing self-awareness is:

PERIS, Frederick S. *et al.* **Gestalt therapy: excitement and growth in the human personality**. Harmondsworth, Penguin, 1973. ISBN 0-14-021642-1.

The real flavour of gestalt therapy is best obtained from working transcripts in the following two books:

PERLS, Frederick S. **Gestalt therapy verbatim**. Lafayette, Calif., Real People Press, 1969. ISBN 0-911-22602-8.

SIMKINS, James S. **Gestalt therapy mini-lectures**. Calif., Celestial Arts, 1976. ISBN 0-89087-170-1.

For those who want a book of self-awareness exercises:

STEVENS, John O. **Awareness: exploring, experimenting, experiencing**. Lafayette, Calif., Real People Press, 1971. ISBN 0-911-22611-7 (pblc).

For those interested in the use of fantasy, imagery and art in gestalt:

ZINKER, J. **Creative process in gestalt therapy** N.Y. Vintage Books, 1978.

On encounter groups, books by two of the major figures are:

SCHUTZ, William C. **Joy: expanding human awareness**. Harmondsworth, Penguin, 1973. ISBN 0-14-021641-3.

SCHUTZ, William C. **Elements of encounter**. Big Sur, Calif., Joy Press, 1973. ISBN 0-913-66202-X.

ROGERS, Carl. **Encounter groups** Harmondsworth, Penguin, 1973. ISBN 0-14-021660-X.

An authoritative and well-written account of bioenergetics by one of its pioneers is:

LOWEN, Alexander. **Bioenergetics**. Harmondsworth, Penguin, 1976. ISBN 0-14-004322-5.

The most popular of books on co-counselling has some variants from the John Heron approach and is based on the psychology of Karen Horney. It is unusually presented in strip-cartoon, but that does not make it any less thorough and searching.

SOUTHGATE, John, Randall, R. and Tomlinson, F. **The barefoot psychoanalyst**. Epping, The Association of Karen Horney Psychoanalytic Counsellors, 1976. Burleigh House, Bell Common, Epping, Essex. (limited edition)

A listing of growth centres, training workshops and the programmes of various kinds of therapists is given in the quarterly publication:

Human Potential Resources
Subscription Department, PO Box 10, Lincoln LN5 8XE

Chapter 14

I've read the book: What next?

If you have read the book through to this point, I hope you have learned something more about interpersonal skills and their application to your work in the college.

However, there is a limit — and a very severe one — to the amount one can improve interpersonal skill performance by reading papers or books. Useful though it is to become familiar with some of the concepts and theories in this area of study, and interesting though it is to read about the application of techniques, it does not necessarily help very much in developing management skill in relating to other people. This can only by done by guided or evaluated practice in work and simulated situations. This is not easy to set up. A certain amount can be done by the individual setting time apart consciously to evaluate his performance over a series of interactions. It is most useful in those circumstances if the individual can write down his evaluation. The problem with this is that our own individual perceptions are very selective; however hard we try to avoid it, we are defensive about our own position in an interaction so we may well have a partial or inaccurate view of our performance. Nevertheless, constant and honest self-appraisal of one's performance is the necessary first step.

A second step is to use another person to help in the appraisal. It means finding someone whom one trusts and respects and who has some of the skills of listening and counselling described in Chapter 8. A particularly useful way of doing this is to find someone equally interested in evaluating his performance so that the two people can work together both at the skill of counselling and that of evaluating and improving performance in the job. Co-counselling, as described in Chapter 13, is an excellent mechanism for this.

A third step is to form a group of people in the college who are interested in improving their skills. Such a group can use books or collections of papers as a way into the subject and then discuss and evaluate the experiences of members in their work. If they wish they can set up practice simulations, role-playing exercises or other practical activities. Every college is able to find a person skilled in this kind of training activity who could advise and help, either on its own staff or in nearby institutions. Finally, one can go on an outside course of training in some aspects of interpersonal skills. There are many weekend or one-week workshops or courses around the country and some which run as evening sessions throughout a term or year.

Two warnings about such workshops: firstly, it is essential to find out that the objectives or aims of the course are understood by you and are ones you want for yourself. There are a multitude of different kinds of courses. Their objectives vary widely, from learning how to work in committee more effectively to experimenting with moving into taboo areas of personal behaviour. I cannot over-emphasise the importance of anyone contemplating a course finding out what the course is about. Many courses cannot exactly describe the techniques used to reach their objectives, but they should be able to state clearly what those objectives are. Secondly, it is important to find out if the people claiming expertise and experience in running a course or workshop actually possess them. There are many short courses run by people unqualified or experienced in that area. It does not follow that, because a course is run by or in a college, the staff involved are necessarily competent. Some hard questioning is in order and would not be resented by anyone who is experienced and qualified.

No general rules can be given as to what constitutes reasonable experience or ability. It has to be left up to the commonsense of the enquirer. However, anyone who is conducting transactional analysis courses should be a member of the Institute of Transactional Analysis and the ITA is anxious that people write to the secretary to check whether such a person is qualified to do what he claims. Similarly, anyone organising and acting as leader to a T-group would probably be trained either through the Group Relations Training Association or the Tavistock Institute. If in doubt it is probably most useful of all if a prospective member can talk to people who have been members on previous courses.

One can safely assume professional competence in courses on interpersonal skills organised by or formally approved by:

> The British Association for Counselling
> The Group Relations Training Association
> The Institute of Transactional Analysis
> British Association for Commercial and Industrial Education (BACIE)
> The Tavistock or Grubb Institutes
> The Association of Humanistic Psychology

Many colleges run very successful courses and it would be invidious to single out any name. Similarly there are many thriving growth centres. The Further Education Staff College has run interpersonal skills workshops for FE staff at between one to two year intervals and invites fully skilled and qualified people to help run the workshops.

USEFUL ADDRESSES

The Association of Humanistic Psychology, Ms. A. Roslyn Madden, 5 Layton Road, LONDON N11.

The British Association for Commercial and Industrial Education, 16 Park Crescent, LONDON W1.

The British Association for Counselling, 37a Sheep Street, Rugby, WARWICKSHIRE.

The Gestalt Association, Beverley McGavin-Edwards, 11 Weech Road, LONDON NW6.

The Group Relations Training Association, Walter Truman Cox Esq., 1 Gentian Close, BIRMINGHAM B31 1NN.

The Grubb Institute of Behavioural Studies, Cloudesley Street, LONDON N1 0HU.

The Human Potential Research Project, Ms. Diana Lomax, Adult Education Department, University of Surrey, GUILDFORD.

The Institute of Transactional Analysis, BM Box 4104, LONDON WC1N 3XX.

The Tavistock Institute of Human Relations, 102 Belsize Lane, LONDON NW3.